A glimpse of how God has worked
through evangelicals in Italy
based on the 50-year ministry of
Arthur and Erma Wiens and their colleagues

The greatest work of God in Italy was not done among the rich and mighty, but one on one, by a man under house arrest chained to a Roman guard.

That's the way God works! In surprising, exciting, and marvelous ways, He is still drawing people to himself in this land of searching hearts.

ITALY

LAND OF
SEARCHING HEARTS

Evelyn Stenbock-Ditty

Christian Focus Publications

ISBN 185 792 606 4

Published in 2000 by
Christian Focus Publications,
Geanies House, Fearn, Ross-shire,
IV20 1TW, Great Britain

Cover design by Owen Daily

Contents

Acknowledgments

Any biographer would feel blessed to have had the level of cooperation of his subjects that I have enjoyed. In a very true sense of the word, Arthur J. Wiens is co-author of this book, giving hours to share memories on cassette, by phone, by e-mail, and by providing diaries, letters, articles and all other material needed to write the story. I am grateful to the Wiens children, Shirley Simonini, Gloria Pieri, and Daniel Wiens for allowing me to scrutinize and publicize their family history. 'Aunt' Betty Jabs has been a valuable resource person, and Erma's sister Ruth Plato has provided personal family information through cassettes, scrapbooks, letters, and photos. This is their story, and I'm honored to have had the privilege of writing it all down.

To the Wiens' missionary colleagues and to Italian believers who sent testimonies for the book, I owe a great debt of gratitude to you, because you are the heart and soul of the story. To God be the glory!

Mrs. Don P. Shidler and Vivian Bauers were alert and helpful manuscript readers. My thanks to Ina Bell for clerical assistance and to Ron Zuercher, GMU artist, for support and technical assistance. Once again, Gospel Missionary Union opened their archives to me, with articles on Italy in *The Gospel Message* from 1949 through 1980.

Much introductory material was drawn from Art Wiens' Master's thesis, 'A Historical Survey of Missionary Work in Italy', (July 1950). Thanks to Philip Schroeder for the use of his paper, 'Church Growth Survey of the Modena Churches in Northern Italy', to Helen Clare Smith for the use of her unpublished manuscript 'The Modena Four', and to Art Wiens for the transcript of a testimony by Richard Ford telling his life story.

My background reading about Italy was made possible by 'Talking Books' based at the Topeka, KS Public Library and the American Printing House for the Blind. I extend my gratitude to the dedicated volunteer readers whose efforts allow visually handicapped book lovers to keep on reading!

Evie Stenbock-Ditty
Kansas City, KS

Foreword

Art and Erma Wiens, Christ's ambassadors to Italy, were the true prototype of those who led the way in missionary work in Europe following World War II. Art was a gifted personal worker who, in his charming and winsome way gave out thousands and thousands of pieces of literature all over Italy. Erma was vivacious and outgoing with a very alert and quick mind. She was always working on some project and seemed to be able to concentrate on several things at once. At a conference where all missionaries in Europe under Gospel Missionary Union gathered for prayer, fellowship and encouragement, there was Erma doing at least three things at once: translating Christian material from English to Italian, knitting and also listening to whoever was speaking in English in the podium. Erma spoke perfect Italian and always with a flurry of Italian gestures with her arms and hands.

Art, on the other hand, was not bothered by the fact that he spoke with a heavy American accent or that he didn't always speak perfect Italian. What was certainly true was that he spoke the language fluently and he spoke from the heart. And God used his enormous but simple ministry of personal evangelism in a significant way. Art was unique. Several factors contributed to build his ministry which had a far-reaching impact on the work in Italy.

Art was first and foremost a man of prayer. In the early hours of the day and any time he could find he would address the Heavenly Father and present his many petitions. Long lists of petitions. He began his prayer ministry early in his career, in college when he began to pray specifically and by name for every member of his class at Wheaton College and then following them in prayer, meticulously in great detail throughout their careers.

Art was a man of vision. He was consumed with a vision and it motivated him during his long ministry in Italy. He carried this vision to others wherever he went. Once while visiting Columbia Bible College (now Columbia International University), during a rare snow storm in South Carolina, Art's car slid into a ditch and some students from the college helped to push him out of the ditch. As they were pushing the car the students heard Art start to tell them about Italy and how much they need more personnel over there. One student wondered out loud if Art ever stopped talking about Italy. Probably not.

Art was also driven by his belief that God would bless the Word of God if he could just get it into the hands of the people of Italy. Art and Erma developed over the years a truly remarkable literature ministry and oversaw the production and printing of significant books, some of them proven study books in English which were then translated into Italian by Art's Italian partners in the work. Art was able to raise many thousands of dollars in the U.S. and Canada for these literature projects. One of their favorite projects was the Christian Calendar project which yearly was widely distributed throughout Italy among believers and non-believers alike.

Art and Erma were also concerned that their enormous efforts could result in churches which were led by Italians and which belonged to the Italian believers without strong dependence on American resources. Early on in their work in Modena they teamed up in partnership with Italian brothers who shared their faith and doctrinal position and who could take the leadership of the church in Modena. Art and Erma were the heart and soul of the work but out front, at the visible point of contact with Italian people were these Italian leaders whom Art and Erma championed and set forth in the work. This partnership was the foundation of a solid, indigenous work, ethnically sound with roots in the Italian cultural soil.

It became inevitable that the Wiens family was more at home in Italy than in America. Their three children all had opportunity to be trained in the U.S. and all three earned degrees in the country where they officially became citizens. But in their hearts they were Italians and today live in Italy. For Art and Erma who gave so much of themselves for the work in Italy and its people, this was just fine with them.

When Erma died in 1996 there was the expected outpouring of love and affection from the Italian people who knew and loved her and respected her for her consistent life of dedication to Christ. God gave Erma enormous grace during her suffering with cancer and she radiated a deep abiding faith in Christ's love and in His sovereignty. The Apostle Paul wrote to the Thessalonians, 'You know what manner of men we were among you' (1 Thess. 1:5). Paul and his fellow missionaries modeled Christianity before the men and women of Thessalonica which made it possible, as the Spirit opened their hearts for them to understand and accept the gospel. Art continues on in that same way in his retirement years, living the gospel before the Italian people.

I believe this book which takes the reader into the inner workings of gospel work in Italy will help in the understanding of the challenge of Europe as a mission field, one where many people may be rejecting the gospel without having understood its message and without really being exposed to its teachings. Many have never even seen or

11

handled a Bible. But they don't feel institutional religion is relevant. Art and Erma gave their lives to make the gospel more relevant to as many people as possible in Italy.

James W. Taylor
Former Vice President for Field Ministries –
Europe and Africa
Gospel Missionary Union

Preface

When I was at Wheaton College in 1946 I became aware of a group of earnest students on the campus who met together to pray for those who were interested in missionary service. On a few occasions I joined those prayer times. There was a profound earnestness in the man who seemed to be the leader of the group. As I watched him from a distance I noted his quietness, his courtesy, a certain grace that set him apart from the rest of us. I had not met him as yet, but a fellow student named Jim Elliot told me that Art Wiens was one of the many World War II veterans on campus – older than most of us, a man whose heart was set on following Christ at any cost.

Jim spent many a time in prayer with Art, as they pleaded together with God to call students to missionary work all over the world. Art kept records for years, counting over five hundred Wheaton students who had answered that call.

During the war in Europe his eyes had been opened to the needs of countless thousands who did not know God. What follows is a heartwarming story of a man with vision. He grew up in a godly home where prayer was as natural as breathing. As a soldier crossing the Atlantic with ten thousand men he joined the chaplain daily in hymn-singing and prayer.

In God's timing, Art returned to Italy as a single missionary. The love story of Art and Erma (who had made up her mind not to marry!) is a touching one, glowing proof that the Lord knows how to bring together the right people at the right time.

On a few occasions since college days when I have seen Art I have also seen in him what the apostle Paul describes: 'the life of Jesus revealed in [Art's] mortal body' (2 Cor. 4:11).

Elizabeth Elliot

Introduction

Blood of the Martyrs/Seed of the Church

Italy! It has always been there for you, the one country of all the world that you are sure you can find on a map. An airline attendant quipped that to fly from Europe to the Holy Land, 'you follow the boot to the heel, and hang a left'. Whether you search a Bible map of ancient times or a present day atlas, the novel shape of the country jutting out into the Mediterranean Sea serves as a guidepost to locating all other sites in the area.

Nor has Italy changed its name over the centuries. Italy. It is there in Bible times, it remains Italy through medieval times, through the Renaissance, through the Reformation and through ancient and modern wars. Cornelius, in Acts 10, was a member of an Italian regiment of soldiers stationed in Caesarea. Aquila and his wife Priscilla, in Acts 18, were Jewish people expelled from Italy by Claudius Caesar. Marco Polo left his home in Venice, Italy to travel to China; Augustine's mother prayed for her now-famous son from her home in Milan.

Rome, too, is familiar to us from ancient history. A thousand years before Christ the people of the Italian peninsula were hardy farmers and herdsmen divided into rather small tribal groups. The simple organization and local customs of these Latin tribesmen were the seeds of the political and legal system of their descendants. No people in all history has shown the genius for law and organization to equal that of the Romans.

Foreigners from the east began colonizing in Italy earlier than 400 BC. Greek colonists entered Sicily and southern Italy bringing advanced civilization and commerce which opened the Italian peninsula to the outside world. Also from the east, the Etruscans, possibly from Asia Minor, settled in northern Italy. Tuscany, the region around Florence, is derived from the name of these ancient colonists.

By the 5th century BC Rome controlled all of Italy, and as a result of her conquest of Carthage in North Africa, she emerged as the great Mediterranean power. Augustus Caesar (who decreed the census of Luke 2) formed the great world-state called the Roman Empire, which supplied the framework of civilization. God used this mighty empire to fulfill the prophecies of Bethlehem as well as those surrounding Christ's death on the Cross. Romans were present in the multi-lingual crowd at Pentecost. The gospel started on its journey to the ends of the earth over Roman roads. In Acts 16 and again in Acts 22, being a Roman citizen worked to the advantage of the Apostle Paul.

We tend to think of missions as a modern phenomenon, with missionary work beginning about in the 18th century. In fact, the Great Commission has been faithfully carried out by Christian believers from Pentecost onward. The groundwork was laid in Italy, not by missionaries, but by the presence of Jews who came long before the birth of Christ to seek commercial opportunities. The Jews introduced into the mixture of pagan rituals, superstitions, and polytheistic beliefs the worship of the one true God. They sought no converts, but welcomed Gentiles into their synagogues, thus familiarizing the pagans with Jewish doctrines of God, morality, and heaven.

We are not sure who first brought the gospel to Italy. It seems likely that Roman travelers converted in Jerusalem during Pentecost returned home with the good news. In his letter to the Romans, in which the Apostle Paul expresses his desire to visit Rome, he greets more than 20 individuals and five house churches (Rom. 16: 3-15). Quite likely some of these were his acquaintances from missionary travels who had moved to Rome; some probably were his converts. While he was imprisoned in Rome, he preached, witnessed and won many to Christ (even from Caesar's household), as did the brothers who were with him. In the first few decades after the Resurrection the gospel spread widely throughout the Roman Empire.

Contrary to Catholic teaching, Peter did not found the church in Rome, nor was he 'Bishop of Rome'. It is generally believed that he arrived about five years before his death. If so, it is significant that this apostle and faithful witness for Christ would choose to go there at such a dangerous time. The combined witness of so many stalwart believers resulted in a strong and very vocal church dedicated to spreading the gospel with no regard for their own safety. The blood of the martyrs indeed proved to be the seed of the church! The catacombs attest to the millions of converts, who even under threat of unspeakable torture boldly witnessed for Christ in Rome.

The first great persecution of Christians at Rome came in 64 AD when Nero burned Rome and directed the charges against the helpless Christians. Tradition holds that the Apostle Paul was beheaded during that period. How touching to read the prison epistles knowing the setting in which they were written! During what is believed to be his first imprisonment, to the Philippian church Paul writes of joy and contentment, adding, 'I eagerly expect and hope that I will ...

have sufficient courage, so that now as always Christ may be exalted in my body' (Phil. 1:20,21, NIV). He may have been released and arrested again. During the second imprisonment he writes to Timothy, 'I am already being poured out like a drink offering, and the time has come for my departure. I have fought a good fight, I have finished the race, I have kept the faith' (2 Tim. 4:6, 7, NIV).

Peter's epistles, too, inspire a sense of awe and gratitude for his confidence in God's care during life's stressful ordeals. Suffering saints in Rome and throughout the ages have been comforted and strengthened in the faith by the inspired writings of Peter and Paul. Church historians Eusebius and Jerome both accept the tradition that Peter was martyred in Rome.

The suffering of Christians in Nero's time is described as mockery of every sort. They were covered with the skins of animals, they were torn by dogs and perished, or were nailed to crosses, or were doomed to the flames and burned. As many as 500 Christians a night were killed and used as human torches to light the evening entertainment, even in Nero's garden. The ruins of the Coliseum stand as a reminder of atrocities against Christians too cruel for the sensitive heart to hear.

In all, ten great persecutions covered the first 300 years of Christianity. The last of these, during the reign of Diocletian and his successors from 303 to 310 AD, included edicts ordering every copy of the Bible to be burned and for Christians not renouncing their faith to be stripped of their citizenship. The baths of Diocletian were erected by forced labor of enslaved Christians suffering for their faith.

Persecution of Christians abated with the emperor Constantine's Edict of Toleration, issued in Milan in 313 AD. The edict did not make Christianity the state religion of the

Roman Empire, nor did it recognize the inalienable right of man to worship according to the dictates of his conscience. It was state policy, pure and simple, designed to promote public peace and security.

Many of the aristocracy in Rome had always clung to their pagan gods. Italian peasants had not given up superstitious cults. Because the Roman Church had been so corrupted by paganism, Constantine moved the church headquarters from Rome to Constantinople (now Istanbul, Turkey). One of his great maxims was that the emperor is *in* the church, not *over* it.

Theodosias (379-395) declared Christianity the religion of the empire, making church membership compulsory. When the Roman world swarmed into the church for its benefits and blessings, pagan superstitions and substitutions for gospel truth entered as well. Over the centuries, the Roman Catholic Church, which claims equal authority with the Bible and the Pope infallible, adopted these practices, some of which can be traced back to early, pre-Christian Italian customs. Infant baptism as a means of purification is an old Italian practice; holy wells as healing places, exorcism for the protection of beasts, vestal virgins (replaced by nuns), and the wearing of charms are all drawn from of ancient Italian customs. Prayers for the dead, the sign of the cross, the use of wax candles, the daily mass, the worship of Mary, the doctrine of purgatory, and the use of relics, images, and the cross were among the many early decrees drawn from pagan religions still found in the Catholic church today.

The glory of Rome eventually began to dim as her wealth and luxury weakened her resistance to the barbarians outside the empire. By 450 AD the strength and beauty of the Roman Empire and of Greece was gone, plunging the civilized world into the Dark Ages. For several hundred years a broken, ravaged Italy searched for some form of rule that would make life more bearable. City life, stable government, common language, and a uniform currency were gone. Bartering and battles replaced them, and it was every man for himself.

Even in this darkest night, the light of the Lord was shining. Among the missionaries who brought the gospel to the now heathen Italy was an Irishman named Columbanus, who took a band of fellow-missionaries to France, Switzerland, and in his old age, to Italy. His missionary efforts were focused on the conversion of the pagans and the winning of Aryan Lombards to the orthodox faith.

Peter Waldo, a wealthy merchant in Lyon, France, taking to heart the advice Jesus gave to the rich young ruler (Luke 10), sold all and followed Christ. In the 12th century, this stalwart of the faith became the leader of the Waldensians of northern Italy. There is no definitive history of the origin of these outstanding Italian believers. According to an old tradition the Waldensians living in the alpine valleys of Piedmont, traced their beginnings back to Apostolic times. For generations they farmed the valleys producing bumper crops of barley, rye, oats, and maize. They terraced the mountainsides by carrying baskets of soil laboriously up the steep inclines to plant vines, fig trees, cherries, walnuts, mulberries, and chestnuts. These staunch brethren suffered indescribable horror in periodic persecution over the centuries because of their belief in the authority and supremacy of the Scriptures, the right of the common man to read the Bible and to preach it, justification by faith, and a life of good works. Their pious lives spoke loudly, and many followed them, swelling their number in every generation. Their disciples could not be silent because of their love for the Word of God and the urgency they felt to preach and testify to others.

20

In 1517, Luther nailed his thesis to the door of the Wittenburg Church in Germany. That same year in Italy, the Archbishop of Turin charged the Waldensians with almost an identical list of 'heresies'. He launched a crusade to annihilate this faithful group of believers. Miraculously some escaped by hiding in the mountains. Finally, in 1655, the most terrible massacre by French and hired Irish troops took place against the Waldensians, using such dreadful cruelty that Cromwell of England launched diplomatic efforts to stop it.

While the church at Rome was gaining in power and liquidating her enemies, the Italian Renaissance was awakening cultural refinement in Europe through the renewed interest in literature and philosophy of the ancient world. We have Italian scholars and clergy to thank for searching out and laboriously copying priceless old manuscripts and, in addition to the Vatican Library, setting up great university libraries to house valuable collections of classical literature. Italy preserved a wealth of treasured works of art and architecture, and many distinguished poets, orators, writers, artists. and musicians were born and educated there. Her cultural contribution to the world is unsurpassed.

Italy is situated in a very favorable location. From antiquity her western seaports, Genoa and Naples, served as doors to and from the expanding world. Mysterious, captivating Venice, Milan, outstanding center of art, finance, and politics, and elegant, progressive Florence stood tall and strong among European cities.

Northern Italy is favored with rich, fertile soil, ample rain, the great Po River and her tributaries, and a European-like climate. Italy, France, Switzerland, Austria. and Slovenia all claim a portion of the beautiful Alps. The Apennine mountain range which separates the north from the peninsula rises in parallel ridges resulting in a diversity of hills and valleys. The Apennines are highest on the eastern coast of Italy, dropping to the Adriatic Sea. The Baltic states lie just 50 miles across the Adriatic. The whole western coast of Italy, most favorable to seaports, is subject to earthquakes and is sprinkled with extinct and motionless volcanos. Mt. Vesuvius on the Bay of Naples and Mt. Etna in Sicily are the only active craters in the region.

Along Italian highways, great cities are linked together by towns and villages, each with its ancient town square walled in by the cathedral, shops, sidewalk cafes, rooming houses and hotels. Streets too narrow for cars wind up and down past homes whose open windows and flower boxes express the warmth of the Italian people. On the outskirts, newer villas and high rise apartments display the modern Italy, her computer-literate children, and technology-wise adults poised to capture the future's best for themselves and their land.

Outstanding scenery in Italy is not limited to the north. Tetrarch, with a companion, is said to have climbed a rock cliff south of Rome to a height thought unattainable. At the summit he looked over the impressive rock scenery and the forests, lakes and meadows below. Overcome by its breathtaking beauty, he pulled out his *Confessions of St. Augustine*, and read from Chapter 10, 'and men go forth and admire lofty mountains and broad seas and roaring torrents, and the ocean, and the course of the stars, and forget their own selves while doing so'.

While northern Italy borders Europe, Sicily and some areas of southern Italy resemble North Africa, much of the land hot and arid. Without irrigation the ground was barren and unproductive, and in summer the heat was so unbearable ancient monks escaped to mountain retreats. Along with poverty, heat, and earthquakes, the eight million people of the ancient Kingdom of Naples endured malaria from the mosquito-filled undrained marshes of the area. Sardinia and Sicily are islands just west of Italy, Sicily almost touching the toe of the boot.

Throughout history, various tyrannical emperors and despotic popes, Italian and foreign, looked to enrich themselves, sometimes subduing, but never uniting the country. The historian Burckhardt speaks of 'corruption in the citadel of holiness'.

In 1861, while the Civil War was erupting in America, a united Kingdom of Italy was proclaimed when General Giuseppe Garibaldi, forming an alliance with Victor Immanuel II, King of Sardinia, conquered Sicily and the Kingdom of Naples.

Not all of Italy was included in the new kingdom. Rome was still a papal possession, and Venice was controlled by Austria. In 1866 under the leadership of General Garibaldi, Venice became a part of Italy. Italy annexed Rome in 1870, when Garibaldi triumphantly entered the city. The pope was stripped of his temporal power, and for several decades succeeding popes claimed to be 'prisoners' in Vatican City. The first civilian to enter by the Porta Pia was Matteo Prochet, Moderator of the Waldensian Church. He bore a Bible in his hand and later preached there. Two Waldensian churches and a theological seminary were established in Rome.

The work of the Brethren had spontaneous beginning in Italy in 1854, when the Grand Duke Leopold II commissioned Count Piero Guicciardini to raise the education standards of the country. On a chance meeting with Lambruschi, brother of Pope Gregory XVI, the count asked, 'Could you recommend a good book of moral stories that I might share with my pupils?'

Lambruschi looked around carefully before recommending the Scriptures. The count searched through his library for a copy in Italian, and finding none, read the entire Vulgate. Observing that the Scriptures were in opposition to the teachings and practices of the Church of Rome, he said, 'Either I don't understand, or we have strayed far from the truth.' As he continued to study his inherited beliefs were shaken.

One day as the count walked down the magnificent staircase of his palace he saw the caretaker slip a book he was reading under the table. He approached the caretaker and asked what he had been reading. Trembling, the man finally pulled out a Bible written in Italian. To his surprise, the Count invited him to bring the book to a designated location so they could study together. Thus began a secret Bible study between the count and the caretaker.

Once when the count was reflecting on the words, 'the communion of saints', it occurred to him that one couldn't have communion with dead saints. He set out to discover what the Bible meant by saints. Finding foreigners who believed as he did, he began meeting secretly with them and with other Italians who were converted. The new belief was spreading, and even though they held meetings in moving carriages, various homes, and other secret places, eventually they were found out. The count as well as the peasants he worshiped with were imprisoned, after which he chose to go into exile, eventually going to England. There he discovered the Plymouth Brethren, who believed as his Italian group did. When tensions eased and more freedom was allowed, he returned to Italy and his groups of believers.

By 1950 there were about 150 Brethren Assemblies in

Italy. They are autonomous gatherings of believers, led by elders within the group. One does not 'join' an assembly. There are no paid pastors and there is no rule from a central headquarters, although the assemblies meet together periodically for fellowship and prayer. In 1950 the Brethren had an association that supported full-time Italian workers, an orphanage in Florence, and a monthly magazine.

Between 1848 and 1929 various Protestant groups established themselves in Italy. Taking advantage of partial tolerance under the Concordat of 1870, Presbyterians from Scotland, Baptists from the southern United States, Wesleyans and Baptists from England, Methodists from the U.S.A., the Salvation Army, Pentecostal, and Seventh Day Adventists succeeded in planting churches. Through the moving of the Holy Spirit, indigenous assemblies of believers also sprang up. The inherent difficulties of evangelization in a Catholic country kept the congregations of all these groups very small, but the seed was good, and fruits of this work remain to this day.

The Lateran Agreement in 1929 ended the pope's 'imprisonment' by making him sovereign ruler over his tiny, but immensely wealthy empire, Vatican City, two square miles within the great city of Rome. It also made distribution of evangelical literature and the Bible illegal.

At last, in 1946, after World War II, the Italian Republic was formed. Italy was united, rebuilt, and modernized, and she prospered. Simply by building dams and draining marshland, building roads and public works, teaching the rudiments of agriculture, and providing education, even the impoverished south was transformed into a valuable area, rich in vegetables, vineyards, orchards, and olive groves. The 20th century finally arrived in southern Italy and tapped into its greatest wealth, the minds of its highly gifted people.

This is a missionary story, the account of what, over a period of fifty years, God chose to do in Italy through Arthur and Erma Wiens, their Italian-born children, and their Italian colleagues. Arthur Wiens understood the country to which God had called him. During World War II he spent one year in Italy in military service. That year opened his eyes to the great need of missionaries in the country. Like so many other World War II servicemen, his college plans were interrupted by the draft. Thirty-nine months later, he was ready to enter missionary training. During these four years of post-war college, the call of the Lord to missionary service in Italy became increasingly clear to Arthur. He was ready and eager to go back.

The stated purpose of Arthur Wiens' Master's Thesis at Columbia Bible College in 1950 was 'to trace the early church's history and continued evangelical history, and the origin and history of the Roman Catholic Church in order to ascertain the types of mission work carried out and to what extent Italy has been evangelized'. In the final paragraph of the thesis he wrote, 'The challenge that comes to me is to find my place in God's program in the training of Italian young people who will go forth as witnesses for their Savior. Within two weeks after finishing this thesis I expect to be on my way to Florence, Italy in obedience to God's command, "Go ye into all the world and preach the Gospel to every creature".'

Chapter 1

A War a Half-World Away from Home

When the sleek hospital ship carrying the 70th General Hospital military unit docked in Italy in November 1944, the country with so troubled a history was still reeling from two decades of the tyrannical rule of the dictator Mussolini. His reign ended only by plunging Italy into the devastation of World War II. In late 1944, fierce battles raged in the Apennine Mountains where victory for the allies would take another winter of hard fighting and much loss of life.

Benito Mussolini established the Fascist League in 1919 after enlisting street thugs to gain attention through muggings, assassinations, and other terroristic activities. He quickly gained popularity among landowners and industrialists who hired him to deal with the Communist threat. In 1922, during a time of internal instability in Italy, King Victor Emmanuel III called on Mussolini to set up a new government. Mussolini became Prime Minister, and in 1925 set himself up as 'Head of Government'. Under his direction and through brute force, his black shirt fascist members disposed of dissenters in and out of the parliament, oppressing members of the Socialist and Communist parties. He destroyed or suppressed all newspapers competing with his own. Before long he controlled all the media, allowing the Italian people to read and to hear only strictly censured news. He demanded that Fascism be promoted in the schools and he eventually forced even university professors to join and promote his party. Fascism developed and changed according to the whims of this tyrant, whose views depended on the atmosphere of the moment.

Increasingly, Mussolini's philosophy focused on war. 'War is to men what maternity is to women,' he said. By 1935 he was looking for a war large enough for him to display his cunning and strength to the world. In a daring move, in 1939 Italy invaded Ethiopia, severing Mussolini's tenuous ties with France and England. Germany invaded Austria, and swallowed up Poland, Norway, the Netherlands, Denmark, Belgium, and France. From southern France the Nazi forces crossed the Mediterranean to occupy French Morocco and Algeria, moving east, while the Italians swept across North Africa west from Ethiopia.

The war Mussolini had been wishing for culminated in Nazi control of Italy, the pulverization of Italian cities and countryside by both Allied and German bombing, the execution of Mussolini by his own people, and the downfall of the Fascist regime.

As Art Wiens was finishing high school in May 1939, Europe was going to war. Since their parents were Mennonites, the Wiens boys had discussed what they would do when called up for the draft. They learned that they could serve in the army as conscientious objectors, taking their responsibility in the war effort without bearing arms.

When the time came to register for the draft, Arthur signed up as a conscientious objector, not because of his heritage, but because of his own convictions. He had twice made a declaration of his faith in Christ, when he was seven, and again at eleven. He considered June 19, 1939, the date of his real conversion to Christ. On that day, he was out in the fields plowing. When he stopped to rest the horses, he took out his New Testament to read. The Holy Spirit used the jailer's question in Acts 16:30 to touch Art's heart: 'What must I do to be saved?' It was as if the answer Paul gave was directed personally to him: 'Believe on the Lord Jesus Christ, and thou shalt be saved.' A month later he was baptized.

Grandparents on both sides of the family immigrated to America from the Ukraine in about 1875, seeking religious freedom. They settled in the region around Mountain Lake, Minnesota. In the early years, Art's father combined farming with teaching in the local school, but the call of God brought about a big change in his life. John Wiens, a graduate of Northern Baptist Seminary in Chicago, attended a conference at Northern Gospel Mission working out of Virginia, Minnesota. The founder, J.P. Welliver, had served in Morocco until his wife became ill. He then opened NGM as a home mission board. In addition to planting churches and filling the pulpits with called men and women of God, NGM served as a practical training ground for Bible school graduates heading for the foreign field.

John and Marie Wiens had heard God's call to take a pastorate. A Swedish girl named Signe Johnson, called of God to Morocco, was completing her practical training under NGM. Signe, a graduate of Northwestern Bible Institute, had been part of a group to carry on a ministry started by Welliver in the little town of Mildred, a farming community in northern Minnesota. They held services in the Mildred school, with a nucleus of believers attending. Signe's heart was with this group, but it was time to move on.

Obeying what seemed clearly the voice of the Lord, John and Marie Wiens left the family farm in Mountain Lake and bought a farm in Mildred on which to raise their family, to become 'tentmaker' missionaries, supporting themselves. Thus, in 1926 when Signe left for North Africa, John Wiens began as pastor of the faithful little group. In 1932, on prime land near the main highway, Pastor Wiens and his congregation built Mildred Chapel. Atop the building they erected a huge sign declaring, 'Christ died for our sins'.

G. Christian Weiss, a missionary statesman who was to be influential in Art Wiens' life, grew up fifteen miles from the Wiens farm. He was from a family of 17 children crowded into a one-room home, children sleeping in the bed, under the bed, and on some rough boards up in the rafters. He loved to call himself a 'jack-pine savage', a colorful way to describe pre-technology depression era country kids in northern Minnesota. Life was casual, rules were firm, few, and understood by all. Whether as a community or within the family, children invented their own entertainment.

The Wiens home was filled with the typical raucous activity and laughter one might expect in a family of four boys and two girls. School activities, combined with household and farm chores, helped drain some of their boundless energy. Completion of chores, diligence in studies and attentive minds in church meetings were the basic expectations.

To the Wiens children, prayer was as natural as talking, eating, or breathing. When faced with a problem, or a need, or a question, the family prayed together. The children learned to listen for God's voice and rely on the accuracy of His guidance by backing it up with appropriate scriptural principles. At home and in church, the value of giving to support missions was impressed on their hearts. Arthur was eleven when the church was built. In evangelizing the rural area surrounding the chapel, Pastor Wiens took the young people with him to testify, sing, and participate in witnessing. His joy in serving the Lord was contagious. During the thirty-two years of his tenure as pastor he laid the foundation for equipping young people to answer God's call. Forty-eight young men and women from Mildred Chapel gave their lives to full-time Christian service, including three of his own six children, Arthur to Italy, Ruth to Japan, and Robert to Mali Republic. Matilda, Harry, and Jim Wiens 'stayed by the stuff', active in supporting missions, in Gideon work, in local churches wherever they lived, and in short term projects overseas.

In a tent meeting the summer of 1939, Arthur dedicated his life to serve the Lord full time. After high school in Pine River, four miles from home, he took a year of teachers' training offered by the high school to graduates. The teacher's certificate allowed the graduate to teach two years in a country school. Art hoped to earn enough money to go to Moody Bible Institute. But the day he was to leave for Moody, August 31, 1942 he was called into military service. Rather than going to Chicago, he headed for Fort Snelling in St. Paul to be inducted into the U.S. Army.

The papers declaring Art's conscientious objector status had not been forwarded to Fort Snelling, so he was forced to clarify that matter, not an easy task. The next stop was Camp Crowder, Missouri, where he and nine other men were called in together to explain their refusal to bear arms. For an hour an officer sternly cross-examined them about their home life, their beliefs, and their lifestyles. Did their fathers hunt? Did they hunt? Did the family have guns in the house? Had they ever shot a gun? When it was over and they stood firm, the officer complimented them on their commitment. He believed they would be a credit to the army. The matter was settled; all ten would be noncombatant.

Before leaving for the army, every night for a month Art went to sit in his car to pray about the future. One thing he requested of the Lord as he faced the draft: that wherever he went as a soldier, he would find Christian companions. From the first bus trip to Fort Snelling, where his seat partner was a Christian, this prayer was specifically answered. At Camp Crowder he saw a notice that a group of men was meeting for Bible study. He attended, and made good friends, some of whom he met again in Italy, and after the war.

Arthur had two weeks of basic training at Camp Crowder. Then, because he was a teacher and had taken typing in high school, he was sent to a six-weeks secretarial program. At last orders came to board busses to the train depot, where the soldiers filled several rail cars. They were told that their destination was California; they were headed for the Pacific. But the train never chugged away. After a long, long wait at the station, their orders were changed. They were bussed back to their barracks. Two days later, they were sent to Longview, Texas, where the army was building Harmon General Hospital. The plan was to teach this unit how to set up a hospital in a war zone.

Corporal Wiens became secretary to an office responsible for assigning personnel to various positions in the hospital (500 enlisted men, 100 female nurses, 50 doctors, and several administrative officers). His office was required to properly staff the entire hospital from grounds keepers and trash collectors on up. Art poured over paperwork as the men came in, deciding which man was best suited for each job. Trained people were easy. Others seemed suited to work as technicians or other positions which required short-term training. He filled each position subject to his superior's approval.

His company, the 70th General Hospital, was in Longview ten months, and during this time he prayed and pondered, looking for the most suitable place for himself. They were nearing departure when the Protestant chaplain Robert McFarlane arrived. McFarlane, a high-ranking officer, had been a pilot in World War I and knew firsthand what the boys would be facing. He wanted to be there for them, to encourage them, to comfort them, and to point them to Christ. As soon as Art met the chaplain, he liked him, and McFarlane was also impressed with the outgoing young Christian corporal. Art knew he had found his place. At his request he was transferred to the office of the Protestant chaplain. He worked 29 months as chaplain's assistant under seven different Protestant chaplains.

General Dwight D. Eisenhower was Commander-in-Chief for the Allied invasion of North Africa. With the help of French resistance forces they freed Morocco and Algeria, and pushed eastward, fighting and gaining ground through tedious battles in desert sands. At last the Allies were in Tripoli, poised to cross the Mediterranean Sea where they fought their way into Sicily and entered a long, hard conflict to free Italy from Nazi control.

The 70th General Hospital crossed the ocean from New York to Oran, Algeria, in a convoy of 80 ships, one the largest convoys ever to cross the Atlantic. Their ship, the *Alexander Bell*, was packed with 10,000 men, who ate and slept in 12-hour shifts. Keeping up the soldiers' morale was the chaplain's responsibility, so each day during the 10-day crossing he and Arthur gathered a few Christian men and women, and moved from spot to spot on the deck with their little pump organ. In each area on the huge ship the group led in singing familiar hymns. The chaplain gave a devotional meditation, followed by prayer.

In the security of the convoy, the *Alexander Bell* crossed the Atlantic without incident and docked in Oran on September 3, 1943. News came later that after entering the Mediterranean, some ships had been sunk, torpedoed by enemy submarines.

The 70th General was part of a hospital complex ten miles out of Oran, with three large general hospitals and three small station hospitals sprawled over harvested grain fields. The men of the 70th were given two months to set up a 2,000-bed hospital to receive wounded soldiers from Salerno, Italy, where the battles were raging. They were assigned to a field on which the plowed ground was uneven and covered with sharp stubble. They found spots for their sleeping bags. The next day a huge tent city began to take shape.

The Allies had successfully invaded the island of Sicily, moving into mainland Italy through Salerno and were now pushing into the Apennine Mountains. Casualties were heavy, with both wounded and shell-shocked American boys. Even before the hospital was ready, wounded soldiers from Italy began to pour in. Arthur's duties were to take care of the chaplain's tent, to assist with the services, to drive the chaplain's jeep (and guard it, in hostile areas) and to serve as his secretary. In his spare time he went bed to bed visiting, distributing Gideon New Testaments to those who wanted one. He was to be available in the chaplain's office (a tent, in Algeria) to consult with any who came for help, so he slept there. He and the chaplain both visited the sick and wounded, especially the critically ill. Because morale continued to be a top priority, the officers took the chaplaincy services seriously, considering them vital.

Busses were provided to take soldiers to a Red Cross center in Oran, but many men were uncomfortable in the strange foreign city, preferring to stay on base in their spare time. Many wounded men could not go to the city, but they could be brought by wheelchair to the chapel. Arthur and his Christian buddies began to fill each evening with chapel activities. Sundays the Protestant chaplain held a morning church service, and Wednesdays a midweek service.

34

Monday nights the Servicemen's Christian League, to which various speakers were invited. Tuesday nights the Christians held an Old Testament Bible study, with a New Testament study on Thursday nights. Friday night was choir practice, and they developed a fine choir. Prayer meetings gave the wounded men an outlet to publicly thank God for sparing their lives, and to pray for healing for themselves and each other. The chaplain's tent became a late-night hangout for hospital personnel, ending in a trip to the mess hall for a midnight meal. Art developed into a night owl, with a penchant for late night snacks.

When he could, Arthur took the jeep into Oran, looking for local Christian groups. On a street in Oran the first day, he met an officer with a Bible under his arm. He saluted, and then asked about the Bible. Bill Henderson was indeed a Christian. He was headed for a Jewish mission and invited Art to go along. Despite the war, other such groups were carrying on their ministries in Oran as well.

Moving around the beds of the field hospital became second nature to Arthur, whose sensitive heart and spiritual gifts eased him into his hospital role as he followed and assisted his mentor, Robert McFarlane. In addition to the wounded from the terrible fighting of the Italian invasions, they received 500 young men, 18 and 19-year-olds, suffering from shell-shock, brought in from Italy to fill the mental wards where they awaited transfer to the U.S. These boys were suicidal and filled with mental anguish from horrors of war too great for their young minds to bear.

In November 1944, Art's unit of the 70th General dismantled their desert hospital in Algeria and boarded a beautiful, almost luxurious hospital ship headed for Naples. The GIs' favorite pastime, griping, ceased for those three days at sea! By mid December they were set up in a vacated army camp in Pistoia, where the war was continuing with fury. The facilities were much better than in Oran, but with the awful battle sounds, their work was more stressful. That second Christmas day, the Nazis, taking advantage of their knowledge that many American soldiers would be drunk from celebrating the holiday, launched an attack so close to the hospital that shrapnel fell into the building, wounding patients. Only a platoon of American tanks coming between the 70th and the front lines saved the hospital from more serious damage.

During the 1990's, Senator Bob Dole, a nationally known United States politician with a paralyzed right arm stood as a visual symbol of the millions of brave young men who fifty years earlier had laid down their youth and many, their lives, to free the oppressed half a world away from home. The fighting in the mountains that bitterly cold winter of 1945 was strenuous, fought one mountain and one hill at a time. The Nazis were dug in with the advantage of looking down on their pursuers from various lofty hideouts. Allied troops – soldiers from many countries – struggled up and down the final few miles of northern Italy's mountainous terrain. They were forced to battle through the famed Gothic Line stretched across the peninsula protecting the vital Po River Valley. They were bombarded by Nazi troops boasting of dreaded tanks and artillery and it seemed there was no way through.

Bob Dole lost the use of his right arm when he was hit by German shrapnel. Unable to call for help lest the Germans hear him and return, he lay in a pool of his own blood. Toward evening he heard Italian voices and called for help. He was taken to an Italian shopkeeper's home, where the family cared for him and sent for American medics who took him to the 70th General Hospital in Pistoia.

During the last big battle that took place, the 70th General crew worked nonstop for three days and three nights. At such times Arthur worked on, too, helping where he could, driving the ambulance or helping the records unit with the mountains of detailed papers necessary to keep track of those wounded and killed.

In the twenty-seven months the 70th worked outside the United States they took care of an estimated 45,000 patients. Even with these large numbers, the lives of most wounded could be saved if they were brought to the hospital in time. In addition to the wounds of war, venereal diseases were rampant and soldiers were involved in many auto accidents. Winter fighting in Italy brought men with trench foot, caused by living in foxholes day and night in wet socks and boots. Many men suffered frozen feet in the mountains of Italy. Most of the men brought in were severely wounded, many arriving more dead than alive.

Picking up the broken pieces of humanity after a battle requires a compassionate heart, a stomach of iron, and an objective mind-set. Neither hospital corpsmen nor chaplains have typically spoken about the suffering that surrounded them or their role in caring for the wounded and dying during the horrors on all fronts in World War II. Arthur turned his free-time attention to fellowship with local believers, considering their presence a gift from the Lord to restore his soul and give him new grace for each day.

One incident that he does speak about is that of a German soldier found by the side of the road near Pistoia. The soldier's legs had been blown off, and when he was brought in he needed a transfusion immediately to save his life. All servicemen wore engraved dog tags bearing pertinent information, including their blood type. Arthur's matched that of the German, so he laid down and put out his arm.

When it was over, the German opened his eyes, realized what the American had done, and took a purple heart ribbon off what was left of his uniform. 'I have nothing else to give you in thanks for what you have done,' he said weakly. And he insisted Arthur take it. Arthur smiles as he recalls the incident. 'I was probably the only allied soldier decorated by the enemy,' he says.

And on one occasion, it was reported to the chaplain that ninety soldiers had been hastily buried in a temporary cemetery. Arthur accompanied the chaplain to the grave site and one by one, they stopped by each grave to read scripture verses and pray for the family of the deceased. It was the duty of the chaplain's secretary to then write a letter to each man's family. The form letter said that they could be proud that their son/husband/father had given his life for his country. Art's heart ached for the families. He wished he could word that differently.

Italian cities and towns were largely destroyed by bombing, with surviving family members crowded into whatever shelter they could find among the rubble. Hungry people lined the gates of army camps waiting for handouts of food left over from the mess halls. Many soldiers ate only part of their ample meals, and brought the remainder to the Italians. Collections of food and clothing were stretched as far as possible. In his free time, Arthur drove the chaplain's jeep around – a large white cross painted on it – with helpers distributing chocolate and other items donated by soldiers who kept the chaplain's office well stocked.

One of the favorite hangouts for the Christians in Art's unit was the home of Alfredo Del Rosso, an Italian holiness preacher who lived in Florence. Pastor Del Rosso held a Friday night Bible study in his home each week, attended by both Italians and American soldiers. The Del Rosso's was second home to many of the men, as was the Cavazzutti home across the street. Gaspare Cavazzutti was a retired Methodist minister ninety years old, who spoke some English. When the Bible study grew too big for the Del Rosso home, they held it at the Cavazzutti's, and when Alfredo was traveling, his wife could lead the study. They were devout Christians, wonderful friends to the American boys away from home.

When the war ended in Europe in April, there were a million soldiers from Allied countries in Italy. Men in good health with service time remaining were deployed to the Pacific, where the war with Japan raged on for the rest of the summer. Other front line soldiers were sent home first, ahead of the support services. Arthur's unit stayed on about six months after the war was over. During the postwar period, he and then Chaplain Palmer visited Italian churches all over the area surrounding Pistoia.

One morning the chaplain said, 'We don't have much to do today; why don't you run over to the Del Rosso's to see if they need anything?'

About eight in the morning, Arthur knocked on the Del Rosso door. He found them on their knees praying. Their only son was a Fascist, and he had been placed in an American concentration camp near Pisa, about sixty miles from Florence. They had neither seen nor heard from him. Family was not allowed to visit, and they had no way to contact the boy, so they had spent the entire night on their knees, asking the Lord to allow them to see their son.

'I have the jeep,' exclaimed Arthur. 'I'll take you!' He and Pastor Del Rosso drove to the concentration camp, where after numerous tries, Arthur was at last allowed to bring the Italian pastor in to see his son. Italians express their emotions with zesty hugs and kisses, so both the father and Arthur were embraced by the happy young prisoner. Their report back to the family put the mother's heart at ease. Americans took care of their prisoners, and the son was incarcerated, but healthy and well fed.

Before the rest of the unit was ready to pull out, Arthur was asked to accompany a critically ill patient by train to Naples, where he could get passage home more quickly. With only a day to pack, Arthur grabbed his belongings and began to distribute them to Christian friends in the area. He was surprised that the farewells were so difficult. Deep friendships had developed, and they never expected to see one another again.

He took the patient to Naples, where the young soldier was hospitalized and transported to the ship. Arthur, too, boarded the *Wasp,* for return to the U.S. about three months ahead of his hospital unit.

The converted aircraft carrier's hanger had been emptied out, and 6,000 bunks were stacked six high in the huge hanger area. Ten thousand soldiers packed on board. Again on this ship, the soldiers had their bunks half time, for twelve hours, after which a second shift took the beds. Art was on the fifth bunk up, and like all the men, had to be strapped in lest the ship roll and dump him from his lofty perch. Lines at the mess halls were endless. In their twelve hours up, they ate twice, spending a lot of the rest of their ten-day crossing in line.

Since Art had left Italy suddenly, his family was not expecting him home. No one had any idea how long it would take to muster out of the army, so like most of the men, he couldn't notify anyone of his arrival. The ship docked in Norfolk, Virginia. From there, soldiers from the northern Midwest were sent by train to Camp McCoy in Wisconsin, with a 12-hour stopover in Chicago. The day in Chicago gave him a chance to catch a train to Wheaton College to see his sister Ruth, and picked up an application for the next fall. At

Camp McCoy he received his discharge papers. He was a civilian again!

A train trip to Minneapolis, then a bus to Brainard, where he changed to the final leg of the journey by bus to the Mildred General Store. It was December 11, 1945, and his heart pounded with excitement as he trudged through the snow up the last mile and a half, lugging what remained of his gear. He bounded into the kitchen just before noon to an exuberant reunion. His mother changed the menu to fried chicken for the occasion, and his father, bursting with gratitude, thanked the Lord that his son had been guided and protected through his years in the war.

Mildred Chapel folks had prayed for Arthur, too, and they welcomed him home as a son of their own. He spoke on Sunday, and his father predicted to the congregation, 'I think one day Arthur will go back to Italy!'

Arthur wasn't sure of that. He had loved Italy and had made so many good friends there. He had rededicated his life to full-time Christian service in the Florence Baptist Church. But at times he felt very inadequate, unsure of his abilities. He didn't feel that he was a real preacher, and if he wasn't a preacher, how could the Lord use him as a missionary in Italy, or anywhere else?

Chapter 2

From Soldier to Student

For all the young men and women who served in World War II, military service was a deeply maturing experience. Active duty on the battle fronts etched into their memories unforgettable sorrow, fear, pain, and loss that forever changed their outlook in life. Many received specialized training and work experience as part of their service responsibilities, training that they might never have gotten at home. And despite the negative circumstances under which they traveled, thousands of young people who in peace time would never have left their home town saw the world. The soldiers went away boys, and came back men. Patriotism ran high, and (unlike later wars), everyone felt good about their contribution to the war effort. Americans heaved a collective sigh of relief that the war was over. It was time to get on with life!

Three and a half years earlier, the draft had interrupted Arthur's plans for Christian training. Now he immediately enrolled for the spring semester at Bemidji State Teacher's College near home. To his advantage, the college transferred in the teacher's training courses he had taken after high school, and he was able to test out easily to gain credits in European History and Geography. This gave him the equivalent of a year and a half of transferable credits.

He wanted to join his sister Ruth at Wheaton College for

Fall 1946, but he learned that there were 10,000 applicants for 400 spots. Since Wheaton was out of the question, in April he enrolled for a quarter at Moody Bible Institute and left for Chicago. In a minor miracle, he received a call from Ruth saying that one spot had opened at Wheaton and he had one hour to decide if he wanted to transfer. He dashed over to talk to the Dean of Men at Moody, who encouraged him to go for it.

A high percentage of students were in college on the GI Bill. Art found several buddies from army days both at Moody and at Wheaton. In a prayer meeting one day he was surprised to hear the voice of his friend Bill Henderson, whom he had first met on the street in Oran. They met again in Italy, where Bill was wounded. Now he turned up at Wheaton, president of the Student Foreign Missions Fellowship. Bill urged Art to attend the Europe prayer band. 'It's hard to get people to pray for Europe,' he explained. 'People don't think of Europe as a mission field!'

The needs of Italy were still vivid to Arthur, so he joined the prayer band gladly. Students of the prayer band set about collecting funds for the immense material needs in the countries torn apart by war, and they joined together in prayer for the staggering spiritual needs. Art and others who had been there knew well the spiritual darkness that covered these countries. Daily, weekly, individually and together, the students of the prayer group bathed Europe in prayer. In later years Arthur was to learn that in unusual ways, people in Italy came to the Lord in 1946 and 1947, the years that the European prayer group was intensely active.

As another Christmas approached, Arthur was struggling with a decision. He knew he was called to be a missionary. But where? Did his experience in Italy mean he was to return there? Not necessarily.

Sighing, he went to the campus post office and picked up his mail – Christmas cards from friends and relatives. Then he spotted a card from an old friend in Italy, who wrote, 'Would you come back to work with us when you finish college? We sure do need you!' The next day, another card came from Italy, and the next, in all seven Christmas cards from the area around Florence, Italy, all with the same request.

Was God saying something to him? Was this really the voice of God, or just a natural desire to return to the land he loved? If he couldn't preach, what could he do? He thought of literature distribution, colportage work, other ways he might help plant churches in Italy. It was his close friend Bob Weeber who pointed out that the doubts he was experiencing were probably the voice of the devil, not wanting him to go. Bob encouraged Art as they prayed together, reminding him that he would go in the strength of the Lord. By spring he was convinced that God couldn't make the call any clearer. He relaxed into the knowledge that he was indeed being led to serve in Italy.

And with that knowledge came the desire to help others on campus find the guidance they were seeking. A group of friends began to pray that many from the school would hear and obey the call of God to go into foreign missions. With permission from V. Raymond Edman, then president of Wheaton, they started a 6:30 a.m. prayer meeting to ask God to send hundreds of them out to the mission field. The daily prayer meetings were well attended, varying from 30 to 70 students lifting up the request for God to send out workers from their student body. Jim Elliot, who gave his life trying to reach the Auca Indians, was a fervent prayer warrior in this and other occasions for group prayer. Jim would prostrate himself on the floor before the Lord in prayer, sincerely beseeching God to answer their prayers. And Jim was not alone. All the students praying meant business with God.

Years later in Italy Art began keeping a record from notes in the alumni magazine, and years later, he counted 578 from their student body of about 1,500 who had answered the call to missionary service.

Most mission boards of that day focused their efforts on third world countries. G. Christian Weiss, then president of Gospel Missionary Union, was a good friend of the Wiens family. GMU had missionary work in two South American countries, Ecuador and Colombia, and two African countries, Morocco and the French Sudan (now called Mali). Art was studying for his Master's at Columbia Bible College. As he was praying about which mission board he should contact he received a letter from Weiss saying GMU would help him get to Italy by accepting him as an associate worker. The agreement was that after he determined the most effective way for him to proceed in missionary work in Italy, they would reevaluate their relationship. Arthur could either open a permanent work for GMU, or choose to join with some other group if the Lord should lead in that direction. He gladly accepted the offer. He was required to spend six months as a candidate at the mission, then located in the heart of Kansas City, Missouri.

Immediately following World War II, young people whose careers had been interrupted began to pour into candidate programs for all missions. GMU revived, becoming a grand central station. Outgoing missionaries held back in America by the war were now able to pack and sail. A deluge of postwar college graduates applied to various missions, many being invited to GMU as candidates.

Weiss knew that the aging staff at the mission headquarters needed to be replaced and additional home office help was imperative. He had his eye on a lay pastor in Omaha, a former Western Union executive. Don P. Shidler was invited to come, to be groomed for Vice President of the organization.

Other administrative officers of the mission lived in suburban Kansas City, but Weiss asked Shidler's wife, Christine, to give up her home in Omaha to move into a makeshift apartment at GMU. She struggled with the request. An active pastor's wife, a competent adult Bible teacher, mother of an adolescent son, involved with students at Grace Bible Institute, she had never worked outside the home. Could God be asking her to give up her good life to move to the Kansas City slums?

He was asking that. Assured of His calling, she finally said yes, becoming the only administrative wife to be immersed in the ministry. She was named Superintendent of the mission home. She cared for five aged pioneer missionaries making their home at GMU, and mothered the office girls, who also lived there. Most missionaries and candidates traveled by public transportation, so the Shidler car made frequent trips to Union Station, the bus depots, and the airport.

One of the purposes for the six-month candidate period was to evaluate each individual's ability to get along with others. Did the candidate pitch in as a member of a team, accept the limitations of colleagues, show leadership, handle responsibility well? The candidates helped the housekeeper with the daily cleaning of the three-story building, worked with the cook in meal preparation, and in the print shop (located in the basement). The men did general maintenance and upkeep of the building.

Not everyone appreciated the housekeeping assignments. Like all the war veterans, Art Wiens arrived mature and experienced. Doing menial tasks seem to be a step backward, like an officer returning to K.P.duty. When had he ever painted, or shopped for groceries, or mopped a floor? When he was assigned to paint a room he hoped word of his lowly duties wouldn't spread too far. He begged Mrs. Shidler not to tell his folks. Nor was he good at it. He did such a poor job that the room had to be repainted!

GMU's location was ideal for practical missionary training. Candidates could walk to the City Union Mission, where they taught Sunday school and ministered to poor families or homeless men. The Hispanic community was some distance away, but accessible. The area directly surrounding GMU headquarters had deteriorated into poor white slums, with one immense five-story tenement building right next door. (This monstrosity, dubbed 'the battleship', was the only view from the Shidler's apartment windows.) South of the mission was the African-American community, regularly visited by candidates en route to Africa.

It seemed unlikely that practical service for Art Wiens would be found in his language group. However, someone recalled that years before GMU had contact with an Italian Protestant mission. Just a few blocks north was an area heavily populated by Italians, the beautiful old Northeast neighborhood along Cliff Drive.

When Arthur learned of the Italian work he immediately set out to find it. He was warmly welcomed into the ministry by the pastor, an Italian who had been at the Italian Protestant Mission for thirty years. The mission was Presbyterian, and the church, called Christ's Church, was flourishing with about 300 members, almost all of them converted Roman Catholics. Some of the services were in Italian, giving Art an opportunity to absorb the language he was studying.

The congregation had just built a new church with

educational building and gym, so they asked Art to help canvass the neighborhood to distribute tracts and invite people to church. He was given a Sunday school class of juniors, and a Week-day Religious Instruction class of sixth grade boys. He assisted with the youth group on Sunday evenings and was sometimes the featured speaker. These young people asked for a Bible study class and prayer meeting, so Arthur squeezed one in, finding it pure joy to instruct them in God's Word. He frequently was involved in counseling church kids and found opportunities for personal evangelism among Catholic inquirers in the neighborhood. He discovered that many church members wanted guidance in victorious Christian living, while others were seeking assurance of salvation. Arthur had found his niche!

While he studied, taught, visited, counseled and evangelized, he was also expected to purchase his equipment, which GMU would help him pack and prepare for shipping to Italy. Most missionaries purchased a five-year supply of clothing, household goods, bedding, and other practical necessities. What Art's trunks contained was a massive theological library and what clothing he owned, with a few extra pairs of socks thrown in.

Travel arrangements also had to be made, and he still had a summer class to take at Columbia Bible College, as well as his Master's Thesis to complete. Such a busy schedule fit the personality of this energetic young man who had 'set his face like a flint' to serve the Lord. In May of 1950, the GMU office received word that passage for Art was confirmed on the *Saturnia*, an American Export Lines ship bound for Naples. He would sail from New York on August 17th. The countdown was on – he was headed back to Italy!

Statistics in 1950 showed a population in Italy of 48 million. Of these, one-fourth of one percent were Protestant.

48

Since Arthur had been in Italy prior to his schooling, he received mail from many pastors and missionaries. They all bore the same message as this one from an Italian pastor in Pozzuoli, (the coastal town where Paul landed, Acts 28:13): 'Come! Come! Come to Italy! There is a place for you to preach our Savior and His salvation for our people.' An American missionary wrote, 'The greatest need that exists for Italy is for workers who are willing to sacrifice their all for the sake of the gospel.' Another wrote, 'The need is staggering, so many to reach and so many so ready.' And, 'We need many laborers in Italy and the door is open NOW!'

As the *Saturnia* pulled away from the dock in New York on August 17, Arthur scanned the deck. Most of the passengers seemed to be Italian-Americans going back to their homeland on a 'holy pilgrimage' as well as to see relatives. He already felt like a minority, but early the second morning at sea as he sat on the deck reading his Bible, he noticed another man doing the same thing. He learned that the stranger was a converted Catholic from Yugoslavia, as happy as Art was to find a Christian friend. They spent the trip together, sharing, praying together, and witnessing to those who would hear.

The *Saturnia* docked in Naples on August 27, 1950 at 9:30 p.m. (2:30 p.m. Minnesota time). Arthur's heart was brimming with joy. He fairly floated down the gangplank that Sunday evening, excited about arriving back in Italy.

Bill Standridge, a friend from Wheaton who had been in Naples as a missionary for a year, was there to meet him, and the first place he took Art to was to a coffee bar for *Espresso*. 'I can't drink this bitter stuff!' exclaimed Arthur, shoving the cup away. And he declared he never would. 'You won't be a good missionary until you can enjoy *Espresso*,' Bill teased him. 'You have to learn to drink it.'

If that's what it took, he would do it. Grimacing, Art put the cup to his lips. Within a short time he was drinking *Expresso* regularly.

Evangelical missionary work had a good foothold in Naples. Bill was active in Youth for Christ, which was started in Italy by the Sicilian-born Palermo brothers. The YFC headquarters was in Naples. In 1948 the Palermos had held an evangelistic service in the courtyard of the Jesuit college *Collegio Romano* in Rome, with 2,000 attending and 252 signed commitment cards. Bill arranged for Arthur (the man who couldn't preach, remember?) to speak using a translator at Youth for Christ.

Art had attended the Brethren Assembly in Florence, as well as in Wheaton with Jim Elliot, but in Naples with Bill Standridge, he went to his first 'breaking of bread' service. He was touched deeply. They met in a home in South Naples. The man of the home went to the basement to get wine while his wife took out a loaf of bread. They set both in the center of the table, and just as Jesus had taught His disciples, from these common elements found in every home they partook 'in remembrance of Him'. It was the first of many occasions that Bible times came alive in this land so near the Middle East.

Bill had coordinated an all-Italy missionary conference in Naples to coincide with Arthur's arrival from the states. The conference was an excellent orientation for the new missionary. Of the twenty foreign missionaries in Italy in 1950, eleven – a dozen counting Art Wiens – and several Italian workers met together to talk over and pray together for their various ministries. Getting acquainted with all of these colleagues, united in Christ and working toward the same goal, seemed to the new missionary to be a gift from the Lord. Although they would scatter and work in various cities of

Italy, this foundation of camaraderie would encourage him in the days ahead.

The reports at the conference backed up what Art was already learning, that Italians were eager to receive scriptures and were listening to the gospel with open minds. There were so many opportunities left unattended for lack of personnel. The group determined to pray for fifty more workers in specific fields: pioneer missionaries, Bible teachers, youth camp workers, specialists for women's ministries, children's workers, missionaries to focus on university students, pastors, and evangelists.

After two weeks in Naples, Arthur traveled with missionaries across the Apennines toward Florence by train, with a half-day stop in Rome to see the Vatican, St. Peter's Basilica, the catacombs and the prison from which Paul wrote his epistles. The reality of his task as a Protestant missionary pressed in upon him, exciting and awesome. The stop in Rome lingered in his mind during the remainder of the trip to Florence and beyond, impressing him anew with the reason for the Lord to bring him this far.

And finally, Florence! Home again! How neat to be back, conscious of the hand of the faithful God who had proved Proverbs 3:5-6 true! In September of 1945, in the Florence Baptist Church under the ministry of a U.S. Army chaplain who preached on Acts 1:8, Arthur J. Wiens rededicated his life to serve the Lord. Arthur had trusted in the Lord, and now less than five years later, he was back, a missionary in Italy! Missionary friends hired a horse-drawn taxi to take Art from the Florence train station to the Del Rosso home. He found the Del Rossos well and still faithfully serving the Lord. He also discovered that the Friday night prayer meeting was still going, and some of those who were saved while he was a soldier were still attending. One of his first evenings back he gave his testimony using an interpreter, but hoped 'soon' to be able to give it in Italian.

But first, language study! University classes were to begin November 15, more than two months away. Until he found permanent housing, he learned that he was to stay in the Cavazzutti home across the street, but take some of his meals with the Del Rossos. Pastor Cavazzutti was now 95 years old, but still active. The pastor's daughter, Febe, tutored Italian students in English; she offered to tutor Arthur in Italian for the weeks before school opened.

Pastor Cavazzutti was converted in 1866 at age eleven through the ministry of an English missionary. As a youth he dedicated his life to serve the Lord as a minister of the gospel. In his long life he had pastored more than ten churches and he continued to be an active witness.

The old man's testimony was enthusiastic and he belted out the old hymns from the bottom of his heart. The first Sunday the two went to Cavazzutti's Methodist church together, the congregation saw a beautiful sight, the aged pastor and the young American huddled together on the front row looking up songs in the Italian hymnbook and locating the scripture passages in the Italian Bible. On the way home from church Arthur received another good lesson from his mentor, who distributed scripture tracts to everyone on the tram. The two men had four more weeks of fellowship together. Suddenly, after only one day of illness, Pastor Cavazzutti went home to be with the Lord he loved.

Most people in Florence had lost everything during the war. The city was still being rebuilt and the economy had not yet recovered, so to help support their families, many professional people rented rooms in their homes to students from the University of Florence. American missionaries took Arthur to the home of Dr. Giovanni L'Abate, a chemistry professor who was a member of the Waldensian church. For $2.00 a day Arthur rented a room on the second floor of their apartment. This included the room, his laundry done, three meals a day, and Mrs. L'Abate's mothering care.

Few Italians had cars. Distances were measured by how long it took to walk. The L'Abate home was about five minutes walk from the university.

Not only can God be trusted to guide His children wisely, but He who knows the end from the beginning is also good at picking the best possible person for any given post. He was looking for a people person when He tapped Art Wiens' shoulder, a person who never met a stranger, one who stepped right forward to begin a conversation, and who, with boundless energy and a willing spirit could also keep in step with his heavenly Father, attuned to His voice even on the busiest of days.

It took no time at all for Arthur to step out and look for a fellowship of believers on campus. Long before classes began he located the local Intervarsity Christian Fellowship group meeting twice a week at the Brethren orphanage, a 20-minute walk away. IFES (International Fellowship of Evangelical Students) under the leadership of President Stacey Woods and Dr. Rene Pache, worked to present Christ as the only way of salvation to European university students, and then to establish the Christian students so they could be witnesses in their own universities. Intervarsity Christian Fellowship was set up in Italy at a meeting in Florence April 1950, under the name *Gruppi Biblici Unversitari (GBU)*. The seven Christian students who had begun meeting for prayer Wednesdays at 5:00 p.m., were pleased to add Arthur to their group. They also had a prayer meeting Sunday mornings at the Brethren church an hour before the service. Saturdays at 5:00 p.m. they met for Bible study. The first

Saturday meeting Art attended drew more than a dozen, most of them Christians.

Prayer requests flowed easily as the students became acquainted. One man had converted from Catholicism just two months earlier. His family was unhappy with this decision and made things very difficult at home, doing whatever they could to dissuade him. He needed this support group to deal with his tough situation. Among other prayers, as a group they asked that other Protestant students might be led to join them, that they might be strengthened in their faith, and that they might be inspired to witness.

The Salvation Army in Europe typically had very lively street meetings and evangelical services. As a soldier, Art often attended and participated in whatever way he could. As soon as he was able, he visited this group, as well, so one cold, rainy night Art preached his first sermon in Florence at the Salvation Army. The hall was packed. In the crowd he spotted two young Italian Catholics to whom he had witnessed.

Art's desire from the start had been to train Italians to witness to their own people. Now he discovered one young man who longed to prepare for Christian service. Ernesto had arranged to go to England for studies. As the time of his departure came near, his limited knowledge of English made him uneasy. Studying in a foreign language loomed up as a big challenge to him, and he was fearful.. To help him with English, until he left for school Art set a time for conversing with him and also started him on the Navigators' Scripture Memory Plan in English.

Art was eager to visit Pistoia, where the 70th General Hospital had been located. He invited a new convert to Christianity named Bruno to go along, Bruno was a student from Germany who had converted from Catholicism during his Christmas vacation. He lived in a Franciscan monastery in Florence, but during his vacation he spent several weeks with his aunt who lived in a convent in Rome. All his knowledge of Catholicism did not bring satisfaction, but he testified that everything was so different once he had found Christ.

Bruno went along to Pistoia, where he joined Art in personal evangelism, one man with more experience, but the other with the language. On the way home, the engineer of their train helped the men find seats because he wanted to talk to them. He had been listening to a Protestant radio broadcast from Rome for the past few Sunday mornings, and he hoped they might be able to help him find a Bible. Bruno told him about his discovery of the truths of the Bible and his conversion to Christ, and he went back to engineering his train with a gospel of John and some tracts in his pocket. He asked Arthur to come to his home soon to talk more about the Scriptures.

The Pistoia Baptist Church had recently started a mission in a nearby town. The pastor asked Art to go to this church to preach to a congregation of new converts. The youth of the Pistoia church were going out to conduct services in several nearby villages, and when he went along, Arthur saw the potential for planting solid churches in these towns. And near Florence, Pastor Del Rosso had meetings in five locations, plus he had calls from several other places where there were open doors. The need was so great, the opportunities so exciting, and the laborers so few, that Del Rosso and Wiens put out a letter urging servicemen back in America to return to Italy as Art had done.

Italy was ready for the gospel because to a large degree, youth of the day, all of them born into Catholic families and baptized into the church, were not finding satisfaction in their parents' religion. Catholics, Communists, and the multitudes who claimed to believe in nothing were drifting into a materialistic future with no anchor for their souls. Under whatever religious – or non-religious cloak they chose to wear, there were millions of hungry hearts, promising young people who longed to fill the void with a substantial, elusive something. Christ was the answer!

When G. Christian Weiss came to Italy that November, Arthur was ready to talk over the future of his own work and the ministry of the mission. Italy did need more missionaries, many more. But it was becoming clear that a priority need was for missionaries called to train young Italians to be witnesses to their own people. At whatever level this might be, it was clearly the most effective method to reach Italy for Christ.

The language course for foreigners at the University of Florence began November 15. Arthur found about one hundred foreign students enrolled, from many different parts of the world. All the classes were taught in Italian, a hardship for most of the foreigners that first semester. Arthur remembered some German from childhood and had used it a little during his army days. Since the classes for German-speaking students were scheduled at a different time from the classes for English-speaking students, Arthur signed up for both, which gave him eighteen hours of language study and eight hours of other classes each week.

Being forced to learn Italian for survival was stimulating. Added to this was the mission field at Arthur's doorstep. In a short time he made friends from Switzerland, Norway, Palestine, Pakistan, Egypt, Guatemala, India, England, and the U.S. He also got acquainted with Italian students at his regular university classes. One after another, his new friends heard the gospel and were soon invited to Art's room for discipleship, or for English classes, or to the student Bible study or prayer meeting. His world was expanding.

Before Weiss left Italy he and Arthur spent half the day together at the airport rehearsing what they had seen and discussing possibilities for future ministry. Dr. Weiss had promised to give Arthur counsel, but when Arthur pressed him, he admitted that Italy was quite different from the third-world mission fields he was acquainted with. Finally, he offered three bits of advice: '1) Set up your ministry in an area where there is no other testimony; 2) Italy has churches, some of them old and established. Rather than starting GMU churches as we do in third-world countries, choose the church in Italy with which you can best fellowship, align yourself with them, and build together; and 3) get married.'

Art looked at him quizzically when he mentioned the latter. 'Doesn't that take two?' he asked.

By Christmas 1950, a token answer to the prayer for more laborers arrived in the form of four new missionaries, a couple, a father whose wife was delayed in the states due to their child's severe burns, and a single woman, who moved into the building where Arthur lived.

Chapter 3

The Girl Upstairs

'I have so much to tell you! ... As good a place as any to begin is to tell you how wonderful the Lord has been. When I just stop and think my heart overflows with joy! His goodness is abundant, just wait until I tell you.'

That was how Erma Plato began her first letter from Italy in November 1950. She had reason to be praising the Lord. This vivacious twenty-two-year-old debarking alone from an American Export Lines ship in Genoa had come a long, long way.

Erma Plato had a plucky mother, who twenty-five years earlier had crossed the ocean alone in the opposite direction. Both of her parents, of German descent, had immigrated from Poland. Ewalt and Bertha Plato were wheat farmers in central Alberta. While pregnant with her first child, Bertha joined in the harvest, 'stooking' (shocking) the grain by hand. It was a man's job, but like most pioneer women, she pitched in and worked right alongside her husband. The big garden and canning spelled survival for Canadian prairie people, so no matter how busy or how tired she was, she could not neglect them. She made it through the harvest season. On December 23, 1927, Bertha received a surprise Christmas gift from the Lord with the premature birth of a 3 lb. baby girl. Erma remained a very small child. She walked at nine months and entertained her parents by walking right under the kitchen table.

From the start, Erma learned to help her mother. At about age four, she was sent to the pastor's home to deliver butter, a long walk in the rural area. The pastor's wife gave her a cookie. The little girl (who spoke only German), asked for two more, one for mommy, and one for her little sister Ruth. When they were older, Erma got Ruth into trouble by climbing up on a covered well, and pushing a kitten in. Someone rescued the cat, but Grandfather was very angry. The girls hid in their grandmother's skirts and managed to avoid an old-fashioned spanking, which their mother later said they deserved.

Like Arthur Wiens, Erma could speak no English on the first day of school, and the teacher couldn't understand German. However, Erma was a bright child, quickly learning English along with her elementary school lessons.

When Erma was in Grade 7, a teacher, recognizing unusual talent in the dark-eyed girl, promoted her to Grade 9. She passed her Grade 9 governmental exams and begged her parents to send her to the nearest high school, in Ponoka. It was a sacrificial decision for her parents, since the cost included room and board, as well as books and supplies, but they allowed her to complete Grade 10 before she quit school to work at a local mental hospital.

During this time, Erma, 14, met a 16-year-old carpenter installing kitchen cabinets in the Plato home. She and Gordy Dichau dated some, and when she turned 18, they became engaged. During evangelistic meetings in January 1947, Erma was born again. The change revolutionized her life, because God called her to be a missionary. Realizing she couldn't change Erma's mind, her mother tried to persuade Gordy to join Erma in her new faith. That didn't work. Gordy and Erma parted ways, and much to her mother's dismay, Erma determined never to marry.

In the fall of 1947, Erma enrolled at Miller Memorial Bible Institute in Pambrun, Saskatchewan. She had saved money working summers, and friends helped her financially. She also took Grade 11 by correspondence, a double load to achieve her goals.

Erma felt God's call to missionary work in Europe. Because of her fluency in the German language, it made sense to her to go to Germany. However, someone suggested that with her black hair and dark eyes she would fit in beautifully in Italy. In the end, Italy won out. She applied to European Evangelistic Crusade, and, following graduation from Miller in the spring of 1950, made preparations to sail for Italy in November.

EEC, under the direction of James Stewart, had just begun work in Italy. In addition to an Italian-American woman in Naples, Mr. and Mrs. Stephen Torbico were stationed at Florence. In January 1950, an Italian girl, Maria Teresa DeGiustina, also began working with EEC in Florence. A Bible institute and college graduate, Maria Teresa's goal was to translate six Christian books into Italian in 1950, and she had completed the first, the French book 'The Person and Work of the Holy Spirit', by Rene Pache. Maria Teresa lived at the Brethren orphanage in Florence and ministered among high school and university students.

Weeks before Erma was to sail, she said goodbye to her family. The mission had arranged speaking engagements for her in various places in the U.S. She wrote from Asheville, North Carolina, 'On Sunday I met the folks who are giving me the support, and it was really a joy. The church took up an offering for my passage which was over a hundred dollars, praise the Lord. These people really know how to pray, for which I'm also very thankful. It was a beautiful service led by James Stewart, President of EEC. After I gave my testimony, they had a missionary commissioning service and farewell for me. Mr. Stewart gave the charge and afterward, while I was kneeling in front of the whole group, they gathered around the front and prayed for me, after which they sang, "I surrender all" as a prayer. I will never forget it.'

The next stop was Philadelphia, where she spoke on a radio broadcast called 'Morning Cheer' to an estimated listening audience of 100,000. Another new experience for this Canadian prairie girl was to stay on the eleventh floor of a lush hotel. Telephones were rarely used in those days, so she used hotel stationary to pour her thoughts out to her family and friends, already so far away. About the radio program she wrote, 'I was glad when it was over – in a way.' She described the hotel as 'really swell'.

Erma wrote a final farewell, 'As I face the future there arises in my mind a wide field of possibilities, both bright and dark; and were it not that I am reminded of God's great faithfulness as written in the Word and as found in past experiences, I fear my heart would faint. But even as Moses often reminded His people of God's faithfulness in their behalf in the past, so also I am reminded. Did He not pick me up from the miry clay only three and a half years ago and make me a child of God? Did He not lead me to a Bible School where I was taught His Word in truth, and where in often miraculous ways He supplied my every need? Did He not lead and further direct toward the land of Europe? Has he not already begun to meet my needs toward my departure for that continent? – Faithful is He!'

Erma traveled from Philadelphia to New York alone, finding her way to the port to sail on the American Export Lines *Vulcania*, sister ship to the *Saturnia* on which Arthur had sailed three months before. Friends of 'Morning Cheer' in Philadelphia prepared a consignment of sixty 125 lb. cases of items such as soap and clothing for the poor to be included on Erma's ticket with her trunks and baggage. The president of EEC arrived to see her off, bringing eight red roses. She was thrilled to find other flowers in her stateroom from well-wishers who couldn't be there.

A joke among missionaries traveling by ship or train was that they usually went Third Class because there was no Fourth. Even in Third Class, the *Vulcania* seemed luxurious to Erma, with spacious decks, fine lounges, and an elegant dining room. The food was excellent, some courses very Italian. The theater doubled as a chapel, with a Catholic Mass on Sunday morning. First Class carried many American tourists, but since the final destinations were Genoa and Naples, most of the passengers in Third Class were Italians. There seemed to be so many suave young Italian men, all attentive to this friendly, beautiful young Canadian traveling alone. When a few became pushy, she was glad for the security of a crowded ship, and managed to escape.

After settling into her stateroom, Erma went up on deck to watch the little pilot tugboat lead the ship past the Statue of Liberty and out into open water. The New York skyline faded into the distance, and was gone. It would take eight days to cross the Atlantic, another three days from Casablanca to Genoa. She had time to read, pray and write letters, with time left over to visit with other passengers and to relax. Hours could be spent enjoying the beautiful ocean and watching the schools of friendly dolphins following in the wake, leaping gracefully from the water and flying through the air to plunge in again..

The *Vulcania* docked in early afternoon at the bustling port of Genoa. Erma, excited and somewhat nervous, watched the activity as she waited her turn to start down the gangplank. She slowly walked off the ship into the customs office looking in vain for anyone who might be Maria DeGuistina's father, who was to meet her. She assumed he was middle-aged, since his daughter was in missionary work, and she could only imagine, among the crowd of Italians meeting other passengers, what he might look like. She went through the gates and stood staring around, feeling very lost. New York had been awesome, but Genoa was a huge, busy port in a foreign country. Since she didn't know the language, for a moment she wondered what she ought to do if no one came.

Suddenly a man appeared before her. 'I am Signor DeGiustina!' A wave of relief swept over Erma. She had been found! He spoke in Italian. 'Are you Signorina Erma Plato?' The next difficulty arose. Mr. DeGiustina didn't speak English. Erma took the lead, signaling him to remain where he was a moment, while she went looking for an interpreter. She found a fellow passenger who translated. DeGiustina recovered enough to say he would get a friend who spoke English, and meanwhile she could start getting her baggage through customs.

Luigi, the young interpreter who came, had studied English and had been to Britain, but he was not familiar with American expressions. Erma proceeded to teach him a few. She promised the customs officer that she had no cigarettes or other contraband he was especially looking for. To her relief, he soundly stamped approval on her suitcases without opening them.

It seemed hours before her trunks were lifted from the ship. They had to be opened, but after a superficial snoop, the trunks, too, were stamped and rebound with rope. It was 6 p.m. and getting dark. Signor DeGiustina helped Erma forward her trunks to Florence by train, and took her to his home. To her great relief, Mrs. DeGiustina welcomed her with a motherly hug and spoke to her in German!

The first evening in Italy was memorable. They dined at eight o'clock, and Erma, hungry from the long, stressful afternoon, was to learn that late evening meals were customary in Italy. Luigi was invited to stay for supper to help translate. The fellowship with these Italian Christians was sweet, and the unique conversation in Italian, English, and German was entertaining. She learned that Signor DeGiustina had been a colonel in the Italian army, but because he refused to become a Fascist, the family had lost everything. After dinner Mrs. DeGiustina served tea in a den, where they helped Erma weigh and figure postage for mailing the many letters she had written on board ship. She had become accustomed to the rocking of her cradle at sea, but when they sent her to bed she was so tired she fell asleep without even thinking about it.

The train trip from Genoa to Florence took six hours, an eternity for this bundle of energy who quickly tired of inactivity. The third class compartments held eight people, but usually only two to four at a time joined her during the trip. She had learned four Italian words, not a whole lot of help in breaking the boredom with conversation.

Erma took a horse-drawn carriage from the train station to the address she had been given, the Brethren orphanage for boys. She had been told she would be staying there during language study, and Maria DeGiustina was waiting for her. Maria Teresa kissed her on both cheeks and wrapped her arms around her, welcoming her to the ministry in Italy. The two girls talked late into the night. It was November 25, and the orphanage (like most older buildings in Italy) had no heat so Erma was chilled to the bone and happy to crawl into bed.

How good to hear an American voice on the phone the next day! The caller was Paul Lehman also a new EEC missionary, letting her know that there had been a change in plans. Because the orphanage was so cold in winter, the mission had decided that it would be better to board Erma with a Waldensian woman whose husband, a naval officer, had been killed in the war. She took in boarders and did various odd jobs to keep food on the table for her four children. After lunch Paul came with a little car to take her and her bags to her new home.

As they drove along through the city, it seemed to Erma that everyone in Italy lived in apartments. Except for the few farm houses they had passed during her train ride, she had not seen a single one-family house. All the buildings in Florence were made of stone, three or four stories high, all gray, grayish orange, or sand color. It struck her that the residential area of the city looked more like a financial district or civic center, than a row of houses. The huge buildings were built right up to the street with no yards. Here and there the grass and trees of a back courtyard peeped over a wall – green grass in November, and trees that hadn't dropped their leaves.

Because the houses were all stone and cement with marble floors and twenty-four foot high ceilings, the cold became unbearable during the damp frosty weather of winter. When it was sunny outside, it was much warmer out than in. Few older homes could be heated, but new apartments were built with lower ceilings and central heating systems. Classrooms would surely be cold. Erma hoped she had enough warm clothes at least for the first winter. As soon as her trunks were delivered to her new home, she planned to dig out all the warm things she had brought with her. Everyone was bundled up in woolens. No one wore print dresses or silks, not even on Sunday, so she would pack them away until spring.

Could the Lord really have given her a room in a new

building with central heat? What a gift! When she stepped into the third floor apartment, she saw that the dining room and living room had wooden floors, rather than marble. She loved the place immediately. She was so thankful to have a heated room in which to study that she loved it, too, even before she saw it.

The landlady, Mrs. Fontana, couldn't speak English, but she showed Erma the room. Two single cots indicated that she had a roommate. There were also two little low cupboards with an open end for books, a wardrobe for clothing, a writing table, two chairs, and a stool.

Arthur had been traveling, but when he returned that night his landlady told him that her sister, who lived upstairs, had taken a Canadian girl in as a boarder. She wanted Arthur, who had been in Florence long enough to communicate a little, to go upstairs to translate, since the poor little girl didn't understand a word of Italian.

Arthur bounded up the stairs to the third floor and knocked on Mrs. Fontana's door. He caught his breath when he saw the beautiful young lady by her side. After he helped the landlady with necessary explanations, she offered her living room to the couple, so they could visit and get acquainted. It took just a few moments to discover that they were both evangelical missionaries. Arthur held back the thoughts that raced through his mind. Here was a young woman brought by the Lord to Italy, called to missionary work, brought to the same university for language study, and even to the same apartment building!

Art insists that he didn't fall in love at first sight. 'It took all of 30 seconds,' he says. Erma, on the other hand, was glad for an American friend – anyone who could speak English! She had already discovered a very upsetting fact: young ladies needed an escort on the streets of Florence. This independent, no-nonsense young woman couldn't safely run around alone. She didn't intend to get involved, of course, since she had decided not to marry. Just the same, her letters home spoke frequently of the American missionary who accompanied her here and there, while for several months, Arthur didn't mention her in his letters at all.

Life at Mrs. Fontana's was as good as she had hoped. Most amazing, every morning she had breakfast in bed – *caffelatte* (half coffee, half milk), some buns, butter, and jam. Breakfast was the only meal with butter. Other meals she found a big hard bun lying on the table by her plate. It was proper to break off bites and eat it dry with the meal. Lunch and dinner were served in courses: soup or spaghetti, then a main dish of meat, fish, or eggs, and lots of vegetables, some of them new to her, not found in western Canada. Vegetables were served both as salads or cooked, sauteed with interesting spices or prepared in delicious sauces. If sweet desserts were served it was usually at the noon meal. Most meals ended with a bowl of whatever fruit was in season.

The dessert at the first meal was a bowl of apples and oranges. At mealtime, Erma watched the Italians closely to follow their example. To her amusement, they used a knife and fork to eat the fruit. She described the procedure: peel it with the knife, cut it up, and use the fork to put it into your mouth. She considered the home rather aristocratic, and wrote home that luckily she had tucked her best manners in her little suitcase.

Erma was a charter member of the Church of the Open Door in Ponoka, Alberta, started as was Mildred Chapel, by a non-denominational independent group of believers. Neither of them had preset church affiliations in Italy. Erma's friends from the orphanage went to the Brethren Assembly and came to the boarding house the first Sunday to pick up Erma and her escort. Arthur was no stranger there. He was so blessed by the breaking of bread service each Sunday and the spirit throughout the meetings that he loved to return.

Naturally the service was in Italian that first Sunday. Erma realized that things were going to be very different. She had no idea what was being said during the service or in the casual conversations before and after church. She who lived to communicate and loved taking part in lively conversation was back to baby talk! She couldn't understand anyone, and if she spoke, they didn't understand her.

This was going to be a bigger challenge than she had expected. She determined to use whatever Italian she learned even though this meant stumbling and making mistakes – she called an egg, a grape, and embarrassed herself with many other funny blunders, as all language students do. She could laugh about them, pick herself up and go on. As it turned out, she was a born linguist, and before long almost all of her conversations even with Arthur were in Italian.

The first opportunity Art had, he took Erma to the Salvation Army Saturday night meeting. She was asked to speak the next Saturday, her first speaking engagement in Italy (howbeit with an interpreter!).

The friendship developed very quickly, and before long they were seen regularly together. Living in the same apartment building was very convenient. Her window was directly above Arthur's, so they could call up or down to get the other's attention and talk for a while. The communication became very frequent, at first answering questions about the language or making arrangements to go to student meetings together. Soon it became a reason for a break from study every now and then, small talk, eventually almost every hour.

True to her word, Erma studied fourteen hours a day and practiced Italian continuously. She was gifted in the language as well as diligent. Three months after arriving in Florence, Erma led the student Bible study using Italian. She took one quarter at the foreign language school, and then studied on her own with Febe Cavazzutti as her tutor.

Arthur, on the other hand, had been in Italy six months, but he used an interpreter when he led the study. He finished his first term at the university in February and was dreading the three oral examinations. All exams were oral, and Italian didn't come naturally to him. Although he knew he could quite easily pass a written exam because he had faithfully studied and used the language in all his daily activities, he had difficulty with pronunciation. He passed, 'with very definite help from above'. He wouldn't have to face another exam for three months, and he prayed that by then he would be more at home in Italian.

And he was. That summer, Arthur, still not confident that he could speak to a group in Italian, prepared a Bible study in English. Maria Teresa did any necessary translating. She insisted he knew Italian well enough to drop the interpreter and speak directly to the group. With his security blanket ripped away from him, and with the help of the Lord, he reluctantly consented to do the study in Italian. Granted, still a foreigner with an American accent, he spoke fluently in Italian for an hour an a half, teaching a lesson on soul winning.

Erma began to think about her stubborn decision never to marry, and the quilt her mother had made for her. It was a beautiful handmade double bed quilt. When Erma was about to leave home, she begged her mother to cut down the quilt to single bed size. Her poor mother protested loudly, but to no avail. Erma's mind was made up. She would remain single, and a single quilt was more practical. With a heavy heart Bertha Plato cut several inches off the quilt and refinished the edge. The single quilt fit Erma's cot at Mrs. Fontana's just perfectly. And now?

Sheepishly she wrote to her mother. 'Did you keep that piece of the quilt you cut off for me? If you did, please send it. I may need to sew it back on.'

Bertha did better than that. Happy and excited, she set to work and made Erma another double bed quilt and sent it to her.

Erma described Arthur in a personal letter, 'We live in the same apartment building, so have naturally been together and know each other well. He is a real missionary, consistent and even though he has a lot of education, he doesn't wear it on his sleeve at all.... In one way he is a real American and in another not. He is a real gentleman and yet not the stuffy kind. He is considerate always, not only to me but to everyone.'

In March 1951 she wrote, 'At Easter we attended the mass at the most famous church in Florence ... I came away with a burden.... The old cultural beauty is magnificent and the whole affair is like a concert with the people staring around. They come expecting nothing and they get it.'

In April, friends came to Italy to visit Erma. Mrs. Fontana agreed to put them up. Erma described a Sunday afternoon taxi ride, 'the little carriage, horse drawn, with the little man up front cracking his whip to beat sixty. After that I took them sight-seeing and we walked until they were ready to drop. I invited the other missionary who lives in the apartment below, as I believe I told you before, up for supper.... We had a good truly American time.'

In May she went to an EEC conference in Switzerland. 'It is really humiliating, but I'd better tell you 'cause you'll get a laugh. I had to come back before I got to the border because I forgot my passport! Nearly everyone could think of only

70

one reason why I should forget a thing like that!... The country of Switzerland is so beautiful, almost like a little fairy land, everything is so clean, tidy, and perfect. The waterfalls, lakes, rivers, valleys, snowcapped mountains, trees, and beautifully kept fields with the neat little villages scattered about.'

Italy owns the south side of the famed Swiss Matterhorn, and the same mountain views described above could be found on the Italian side. In June, all the missionaries in Italy went together to a conference held in the Italian Alps, 'right up in the mountains with the rushing waters nearby, so refreshing'. It was only three days.

Later, 'the missionary who lives downstairs has gone to Genoa to meet his cousin going to Africa as a doctor, so of course "the missionary upstairs" misses "the missionary downstairs" – but enough of that. There is no more need of hiding the fact of my falling in love and hard!'

As to Arthur, his letters were filled with the joy of ministry, the many opportunities he had to witness both through the Intervarsity contacts and others he met here and there. His room at the L'Abate home was often busy with visitors coming for counsel, for English study, Bible teaching, for help in Scripture memorization. The Lord was guiding him into a busy, people-oriented ministry, and nothing could have pleased him better.

And although he didn't say so in his letters, best of all, he was no longer alone.

Chapter 4

'Bella Firenze' – Beautiful Florence!

Sunny Italy! But not always sunny. At various times and in different locations it can be rainy, cloudy, snowy, or foggy. As with the weather, so with all of Italy. Quite a wide range of differences can be found between the character of the people from various regions, their homes, their customs, and – important to language students – their dialects.

Bella Firenze, meaning beautiful Florence, was first proudly so called by the Florentines. As time went on, other Italians, and eventually every tourist, traveler, and student who arrived there picked up the refrain, Bella Firenze! Florence was a beautiful city! Although reconstruction was still going on, the city had recovered from the devastation of the war. Even in 1950 it was quite a modern city, with department stores boasting window displays to equal any in America. The average Florentine was smartly dressed. Few were poor, but the cost of living was high. A car was considered such a luxury that the government raised all the taxes of the man who purchased one. Most people used motor scooters, motorcycles, or (most commonly) bicycles to get to and from work.

Ragtag beggars were part of the alluring patchwork of the city. They used canaries or monkeys to entice the passerby to stop, or carried a musical instrument to play for pay. Many beggars, mostly begging by choice, went door to door asking for handouts.

The Mercato Centrale (the central market), a colorful and mesmerizing place, lay between the railway station and the main cathedral. Regulars seemed undisturbed by the shouting and clamor from early morning until late at night. Mobile shops, roofed counters on wheels, lined the streets. The enthusiastic owner or clerk, rarely idle or passive, stood behind each cart, vying for the attention of potential customers. The slightest eye contact, even a look out of the corner of the eye toward their merchandise brought them rushing to the passerby eager to please. There was a cart for stationery, a leather goods cart, a variety store cart, clothing carts, a whole section of food carts offering warm breads, fresh meat, vegetables and fruits in season, and of course, carts with an array of freshly cut flowers.

The University of Florence language school was considered to be the best place for foreign students to learn Italian. Florentines were said to speak the purest Italian, free from dialects and understood by all. Erma's plan was to learn the purest Florentine Italian, and then perhaps move to the south to minister to the needy in the less affluent regions of Italy where the gospel seemed well received.

But, ah! Bella Firenze! What a wonderful place to fall in love! The spring and summer of 1951 were filled with opportunities for witness. A Friday night young people's fellowship was growing, as were the Intervarsity student Bible study and prayer meetings. Arthur, Erma, and Maria Teresa were close friends and worked as leaders, participating eagerly in everything. Most of Art and Erma's outings were with the IVCF group, a very close knit company of Christian students who squeezed many group activities into their limited free time. Since they walked everywhere, the other students would stop to pick up Art and Erma, and they would all walk to their meetings together. Soon the students began to hint that they made an ideal couple and ought to be dating. 'You're both evangelical missionaries,' they would say, 'It looks like the Lord has brought you together!'

Art and Erma didn't need anyone to tell them that they were falling in love. They devised a plan to eat supper together once a week. If they notified their two families that they would be gone, the cost of their meals was refunded. They could get a nice meal in a restaurant for less than the dollar they saved. Arthur, so well acquainted with Italy, also enjoyed taking Erma on day trips by train to various sites. She climbed the tower of Pisa on one such excursion. It was said to be leaning more each year, leaning so much that they quit ringing the bells at the top. An odd feeling crept over her as she climbed. What if their weight pushed the delicate balance too far, or a breeze too strong blew just when they were at the top!

Visiting the beautiful parks of Florence became a favorite pastime for the couple. And for the first time, they found reason to frequent the big department stores. Language students generally shopped at the Mercato Centrale, if they shopped at all. But for rings? For rings they shopped in the elegant stores, hand in hand, window shopping as they went. In May 1951, Erma wrote to a friend, 'Only recently have we thought and definitely prayed about us being together, but now we know it is the Lord's will and we are very happy.'

At a favorite park, by the light of the moon one romantic night, Arthur slipped a ring on Erma's finger. This act of official engagement struck deep chords of love in their hearts that welled up in praise to the Lord. He had worked such miracles in their lives to bring them together. Arthur, who had broken off an earlier relationship as had Erma, was 29. Behind a confident facade he had found it hard to face life

74

alone. Erma, 23, realized that her plan of being a single missionary would severely hinder her outreach. As a married couple they would have a home to which they could invite people, and have so much broader a ministry together. Together! That was what both of them wanted more than anything – to be together. All of their joy that night blended into a deep feeling of gratitude to the Lord.

Arthur immediately wrote to GMU to ask permission to marry, before announcing their engagement. Weiss had left GMU to become Missions Director of Back to the Bible Broadcast. Shidler, the new president was traveling. This left R. J. Reinmiller, the new vice president, with a desk piled high with correspondence, an overload of duties and a shortage of secretarial help. Art's letter was buried for six weeks. Finally, Art dared to write again, just wondering when they might hear. An embarrassed vice president dug out the buried letter and wrote to apologize. GMU was delighted to gain a missionary from a fine evangelical organization like EEC, and the couple could go ahead with the mission's complete blessing.

The next step was to begin the international paperwork necessary for a marriage license. The British Consulate in Florence handled such requests from Canadians. They okayed Erma's request right away. The American Consulate was required to post a notice for three weeks before issuing the approval. Italian paperwork was not only unfamiliar to Art and Erma, but it was extensive, even to producing a paper proving that they were alive! Fortunately the head of the marriage bureau in Florence attended their church. He guided them through the maze.

At last, in July 1951, almost lost on the back side of his form letter, Arthur mentioned Erma. 'The Lord has directed me to my life's partner, Miss Erma Plato ... we would like to announce our engagement.... She will be teaching in three camps during the month of August. My course at the University finishes August 31st.' The wedding was set for September 5, 1951.

When news of Erma's engagement arrived in Ponoka, it was party time at the Platos. Erma asked her sisters to shop for material to make her wedding dress, for accessories, and other items she would need. Bertha Plato baked a traditional three-tiered Canadian wedding cake which they had to pack and ship to Italy. Erma and Arthur's wedding was such big news that excitement ran high crossing several international borders.

The Ponoka newspaper reported an unusual bridal shower, unusual because the bride-to-be couldn't attend. Erma's photo was displayed on a beautiful arch, and her mother sat as the guest of honor under it. The whole event, with an emcee passing the microphone around, was recorded to send to Erma. Several people participated in the program, including three of her sisters. Ruth sang a solo, while Shirley and Bernice not only sang a duet, but dressed as bride and groom to bring in the gifts which had been loaded into a birch bark canoe!

Arthur's best friend was Luciano Petrucci, a fourth-year engineering student from the University of Pisa. They met on one of his trips to Pistoia. Luciano heard the gospel on radio programs from England on BBC, which aroused his curiosity, and when he wrote to the station he was put in touch with the Baptist Church in Pistoia, his home town. The pastor excitedly told Arthur that there was a university student from Pisa seeking the Lord. Arthur soon after led him to Christ.

Luciano traveled the 50 miles from Pisa to Florence every week for Bible study and fellowship. He became a cherished friend, frequently spending weekends in the L'Abate home with Art. Although he came from a Catholic family, his father, a lawyer, was not opposed to his new experience in Christ and his mother liked the changes she saw come over her son. When she heard about Arthur and Erma's engagement, she prepared a traditional sumptuous Italian engagement dinner in her home.

Maria Teresa took over the wedding decorations and orchestrated the reception preparation. The crew of willing Intervarsity volunteers who fanned the spark of romance into a flame determined that Arthur and Erma would have a wedding day never to be forgotten. The chapel at the Brethren orphanage was beautifully decorated with gladioli, carnations, and potted palms and other plants. Even the wall light fixtures were decorated with greens, as was an arch where the bride and groom stood to greet their guests.

They had moved their things into their new furnished apartment, where Erma spent the night before the wedding. At 9:15 the next morning Arthur and Luciano walked to the apartment to get her, and Luciano was shocked to see Arthur greet her with a kiss. With another kiss, (Luciano turning away) he presented her with a red leather-bound Italian Bible. Maria Teresa met them along the way and pinned on carnations. Then on to the courthouse for a civil ceremony, where, with Luciano and Maria Teresa as witnesses, they were married by a Communist government official. He thanked them for choosing Bella Firenze for their wedding and presented them with a huge bouquet from the city. The church wedding was held that afternoon.

Erma's wedding dress was ballerina length with wide eyelet embroidery around the hem, half sleeves, and v-neckline. She wore a short veil held in place by orange blossoms and a veil tiara, white gloves, and white pumps.

She carried a nosegay of orange blossoms tied with a ribbon of white veil. As the organ played the wedding march, she walked down the aisle on the arm of Professor L'Abate.

Maria Teresa, the bridesmaid, wore a rose dress with white accessories. Luciano Petrucci was the best man. And oh yes, there was a beaming groom, beside himself with joy as he watched his bride walk toward him with a radiant smile. Their eyes met, and all nervousness disappeared.

Dr. Edwin Jacques, Conservative Baptist missionary from Naples, officiated at the church wedding, which was in Italian interspersed with English. Missionary friends with him provided the music. After the marriage ceremony the bride and groom were seated at the front of the chapel while their Nazarene friend, Alfredo Del Rosso, preached the wedding message. Because he knew the couple so well, he added personal glimpses that brought chuckles from the audience.

At the reception in the orphanage dining room, Dr. Jacques explained the American custom of wedding cakes. Bertha's cake, beautifully frosted with white trimmed in silver, a decorative bride and groom on top, graced the center table. According to an Italian custom, the bride presented each guest with a little cellophane bag containing an announcement card and traditional white wedding candy called confetti.

Art and Erma were chauffeured by Dr. Jacques back to spend their first night in their new apartment. Alone at last, they opened gifts and read letters. After packing for their honeymoon, they began a lifelong habit of Bible reading and prayer together at bedtime.

The unique privilege of honeymooning on an Italian island in the Mediterranean was not lost on Erma. She was excited the next morning as they left by train to the coast, and by ferry to the beautiful Isle of Elba. For $1.80 a night, they found a hotel room with twin beds, and quickly transformed it into a honeymoon suite before going out to locate a restaurant. The next twelve days they walked sandy beaches, swam, lay in the sun, and swam some more. They climbed to high spots overlooking the sea sometimes following paths that led through tunnels or slipping through old castle gates. They took busses to various towns and better beaches, hiked to lighthouses, and missed the boat for an excursion at sea, only to go the next day.

Onlookers saw laughing, playful young people whispering 'I love yous' in each other's ears, and each day brought new joys in what Erma called 'the first two weeks of a lifelong honeymoon'.

But ever the missionary, Arthur shared the gospel with anyone who would listen. He made contact with two people who asked him to mail back New Testaments. The head of the island's electrical company took them by car to his summer home to meet his wife, since she was the only Christian in her area and he knew she would want to meet the Wienses. They became lifelong friends. The following year Art and Erma were invited back to hold a VBS in a small Waldensian church, the only Protestant church on the Isle of Elba.

They returned to Florence excited about the future, refreshed and ready to pick up their studies and ministry. The new five-room apartment was perfect. The largest room was ideal for student Bible studies, prayer meetings, classes, or young people's meetings. Besides a nice kitchen and dining room, they had two bedrooms, one of them a guest room.

Arthur's GI bill had paid for his B.A. and M.A., plus one year of language study. He would have to pay his own way for the final two years. He applied for a Fullbright

Scholarship hoping to also thereby gain permission to stay in Italy as a student.

When Erma left her mission to join Arthur's, she lost her support, so the first challenge they faced was to really trust the Lord to supply their financial needs. The rent was $70.00 a month. Arthur had support from one church which faithfully sent that amount, so they knew they could pay their rent. A few other donors sent funds regularly, which they stretched to cover coal for their stove during cold weather, postage, and school tuition. The local grocer allowed them to charge their purchases, paying when their check from GMU arrived. Even though they lived frugally, they did have frequent guests at mealtime. After the rent was paid, the grocer's bill often swallowed up most of the check, leaving them living on credit for the next month. They learned to pray for daily needs and for funds to survive from month to month.

Because Europeans cherished education and European pastors were well educated men, mission experts had advised Arthur to get his Master's Degree before going to Italy. Having done that, he and Erma set about diligently learning not only the common language of daily living, but a broad scope of Florentine Italian, hoping to absorb the widest possible understanding of culture and use of the language. They planned to continue in the Intervarsity ministry in Florence while Art took a second year in the foreign language school. The Fullbright Scholarship didn't come through, but the following year Art enrolled as a special student in the Literature and Philosophy Department at the university. This allowed them to stay in Italy as students, and in December 1952 they received permission to stay until July 31, 1953.

Erma's children's ministries with Maria Teresa continued, and when an opportunity arose to hold a vacation Bible school in the South, she jumped at the chance. 'I have to warn you that the conditions will be very primitive,' Maria Teresa told her. 'No facilities, no toilets, no running water. It will be difficult to wash and probably we will have to sleep in the same room with donkeys and chickens. And they do smell.'

'No toilets?' gasped Erma. 'And how do you manage?'

'Well, there will be a container in a corner, behind a curtain. You will learn the meaning of the "vessels unto honor and unto dishonor" that Paul wrote about.'

Maria Teresa recalls, 'I'm sure in her mind Erma was saying a big "mama mia!" And I'm sure she thought I was exaggerating. I added that the people are warm, hungry for the Word of God. It is so much more rewarding to work in the south.

'The VBS was fantastic. Children were saved, women were blessed during the Bible studies, and we were surrounded by love everywhere. And we tasted the best Mozzarella cheese and tomatoes over immense slices of homemade bread.' Coming back to Florence by train four weeks later, both girls were ready for a warm bath and a good shampoo. It had been as bad as predicted. Erma's comment was, 'Thank you for preparing me!'

Erma and Maria Teresa spent August 1952 directing Brethren Bible camps at Poggio Ubertini, and one of the girls saved at camp came to Erma's home for tea that fall. Anna Gloria asked for help in finding Bible passages to read that would help her grow in the Lord, and she said her mother, too, was now reading the Bible. Another little girl, Manuela, was saved at camp. When she got home she told her parents that at the camp they had thanked the Lord for their food before each meal. At her request, the family began to pray, and her mother accepted Christ. The father and another family member were very interested in learning more about the Gospel. Such contacts confirmed the need for a children's class to keep up the camp contacts and to reach other children. Before long, an average of twelve children a week were attending a class every Monday afternoon to be instructed in God's Word.

Floria, a young office worker, was soundly converted at a time when she wasn't even sure God existed. Her ready smile and the joy of the Lord in her heart disguised the fact that she came from an unhappy home. Her father, a drunkard, beat his wife and daughter, and Floria was rarely allowed to go anywhere except to work. Yet she grew in grace by faithfully reading the Word and praying. On the rare occasion when she came to Bible study in the Wiens home she would cry and ask, 'Why does not God answer my prayer and change my family?' Erma and Floria arranged to get together during Floria's lunch hour once a week (12:30-3:00, siesta time). They ate lunch, practiced English, studied the Bible, and prayed together. It became a precious hour in Floria's difficult life.

The Intervarsity activities continued to make up a good share of their ministry. Arthur helped to get an IVCF group started at the University of Pisa, as well as at Arezzo, and he or Maria Teresa went occasionally to encourage each of these groups. A trip to Rome was necessary to get Erma's name changed on her passport. While there, Arthur made some contacts designed to start a Christian student group at the University of Rome, as well.

For Erma, the ministry of hospitality opened wide, and she enjoyed entertaining. Arthur's room at the L'Abate's had been a busy place; now he invited students and other people he contacted to come to their home. When it seemed appropriate, their guests were invited to stay for supper. The midweek Bible study was now held in their home. Many young people were learning scripture verses through the Navigator's course, and the missionaries were working on getting all the Navigator's material translated and printed in Italian.

There was an abundance of secular reading material in Italy and millions of avid readers to devour it. Thousands of books were printed every year, and every city and village had news stands carrying magazines and papers in abundance. Early in his missionary career, Arthur saw the huge opportunity for the silent witness of Christian literature. Even before he was fluent in the language, he was able to find tracts, New Testaments, and other literature to distribute as a point of contact.

After World War II the burden of good sound Christian literature was laid on the heart of Abele Biginelli, an Italian evangelist living in Arezzo. In 1949 the Colportage Division of Moody Bible Institute offered to help him get started in printing Christian books by giving him an initial fund which would help him publish them, hoping to recover the cost by selling the books. Other organizations joined the work, and by 1953 he had printed an impressive list of books familiar to most American Christian readers of the day, by authors such as Rene Pache, Ruth Paxon, F. B. Meyer, H. A. Ironside, and others. 'Christie's Old Organ', 'Pilgrim's Progress', Patricia St. John's 'Tanglewood Secret', and a book on teaching the gospel to children were among them. He also printed many tracts for free distribution as funds were made available, funds from foreign countries, and from Italians who received the tracts.

Several organizations in Switzerland, England and America sent tracts for free distribution, including Scripture Gift Mission, Good News Publishers, Berean Publishers, and Moody Bible Institute. The British and Foreign Bible Society and an Italian Bible House in Genoa provided Bibles and New Testaments. A 'Million Testaments Campaign' had provided 50,000 New Testaments for free distribution following World War II.

Maria Teresa was translating 'On Being a Real Christian' by G. Christian Weiss, for which funds were received to print 3,000 copies. It was decided that to keep providing tools for evangelism and to keep up the flow of good Christian reading, a literature committee should be formed in Florence. Art Wiens, Maria Teresa, Jack Murray, Luciano Petrucci and Abele Biginelli were the committee members, who met monthly in the Wiens home. Mr. Biginelli, who helped start the Intervarsity student group at Arezzo, began a student magazine called Certezze. The magazine, edited by Maria Teresa, was similar to the American Intervarsity publication 'His'.

Into this whirlwind of missionary activities, Shirley Ruth Wiens was born November 15, 1952. Her coming broke down barriers in the neighborhood and spread joy, as people dropped in to see the little dark-haired, blue-eyed baby. Don P. Shidler, President of GMU, visited when she was only ten days old. As he admired her, he said to her parents, 'Now you are ready to open a new work!' Babies the world over have a way of bringing smiles to grim faces and softening the hardest hearts. He expected little Shirley to be a vital key to establishing friendships in a new city. Erma held two vacation Bible schools in their final summer in Florence. One was at Maresca, a village in the Apennine Mountains, and the other at Rio Marina, on the island of Elba. The schools were held mainly for the children of believers, but a few Roman Catholic children came to each school. Both churches were without a pastor, so Art was able to preach and encourage the believers while Erma worked with the children. The VBS at

Pistoia was set for September, since schools in Italy did not start until October.

One Sunday Arthur, with eight others, went to a community 54 miles from Florence, to visit a Christian family that had moved there. They left at 7:00 a.m. by slow train. After two and a half hours they got off, with four miles still to walk. A lad from the family met them at the station and along the way, others from the family joined the hike. It was a cold day so they had a hot lunch ready when the group arrived. They warmed themselves at the huge open fireplace that heated the home and served as kitchen stove.

This family (with seven children) and another family nearby were the only Christians in the area, but they met together for services every Sunday morning. That afternoon, after the guests had enjoyed a country-style chicken dinner, neighbors began arriving for the first evangelistic service ever in the area. The farmers showed the visitors an abandoned Catholic church that was being used for a granary. Arthur challenged them to work toward reopening the church for a place in which they could gather to worship the Lord.

Such opportunities were so numerous as to be overwhelming. Art and Erma were praying for guidance as to where to move after Arthur completed his studies. It needed to be a city where no other evangelicals were working – there were countless places that qualified there. In March 1953 the newspapers carried an item regarding a missionary in Naples who had received orders to leave Italy in 48 hours, so their other fervent prayer was for permanent visas to stay in Italy as missionaries once they could no longer apply as students.

The city chosen was Modena, 80 miles north of Florence in the region of Emilia. Arthur made a preliminary trip and found people willing to accept tracts. Later a missionary couple in Florence with a car offered to take Art and Erma back to make contacts through names and addresses given them by Florentine Christians. On another trip, they decided to visit a group of Christians at Sassuolo, a city of 40,000 about twelve miles from Modena. Twenty-six people gathered in homes for services, one coming by bicycle from eleven miles away. The group was so pleased that the missionaries had come to visit, and they considered their choice of settling in Modena an answer to their prayers.

Although the Wiens family was moving just 80 miles away from Florence, the farewells were very hard. There was the last young people's meeting, after almost three years together. They said goodbye to children at the last children's class, the last Intervarsity Bible study in Pisa, the last one in Arezzo, and the last one in Florence. Goodbyes in various homes, and at the church. The Intervarsity group came to the Wiens home to bring a parting gift, a sturdy, beautiful little bed for Shirley, a very touching gift. Art and Erma knew that the sacrifice necessary for the students to purchase such a bed was a symbol of the depth of their love.

Difficult goodbyes included farewell to neighbors. Two years before it had been hard to get acquainted. Most of the neighbors were devout Roman Catholics who had no desire to be friends with evangelicals and who resented being offered tracts. For a long time the only testimony could be the silent witness of their lives, backed by prayer. By the time they left, the grocer with whom they had done business and the families in their apartment building gladly accepted New Testaments as farewell gifts, said they were sorry to see them go, and wished them well.

There was 'freedom of religion' in the new Italian Republic, but there was strong opposition to the spreading effectiveness of the Christian witness. Even at the University of Pisa, Luciano was publicly challenged by a Catholic student magazine refuting things he had written in the Intervarsity magazine Certezze. The article warned university students not to read Certezze because it was Protestant. Luciano replied to the questions they asked, and some of his answers were published. The war of words was an indication of an undercurrent of antagonism toward evangelicals. It was clear to all of them that by moving to a city previously untouched by evangelical witness Art and Erma would very likely face opposition, as well..

But very good news encouraged their hearts. Their good friend Jack Murray, the Scottish missionary on the literature committee, received permission from the Florence police headquarters to remain in Italy indefinitely. This was the first such permission granted since 1940, and it seemed to be a sign of good things ahead.

Chapter 5

Expelled from Italy!

When Arthur and Erma moved to Modena, 80 miles north of Florence, they traveled by train. From Tuscany to the region of Emilia Romagna, the scenery changed completely, from rolling hills covered with olive trees to the plains of Emilia, checkered with fields of grain and acres of fruit trees.

The province of Modena, home of the Ferrari race car, is situated in the Po valley, one of the world's richest agricultural areas. The city of Modena is located on the main highway across Italy from Naples to Switzerland, about half way between Florence and Milan. In the 1950s it was known as 'the little Russia' of Italy, since the Communist party was very strong there. There was a university, an officer's military training school, and an army camp. In 1953 the city of 120,000 boasted thirty-one Roman Catholic churches. There was also a prominent Jewish synagogue, built when more than a thousand Jews lived in Modena. With the Nazi invasion of World War II, hundreds of Jews were killed, others sought perilous ways to escape, and a few switched religions to save their lives.

The region of Emilia, the size of Massachusetts, had a population of 3,500,000 scattered in many villages, towns, and cities. There were eight provinces in Emilia, each with a good-sized government center. Modena, Bologna, Ferrara, and Parma (home of Parmesan cheese) had universities. In the whole region there were just a few very small Protestant churches.

For more than a year, prayer had been focused on God's guidance in choosing a place to settle, so these facts were exciting to the young missionary family facing their first assignment alone. They left their support system behind them, because in Modena there were no evangelical churches, no other missionaries, and no close personal friends. In their place there would be new people, new challenges, new responsibilities. The day after arriving they wrote, 'We are in the midst of boxes, trunks, and suitcases in our new home, but we want to greet you from Modena and tell you what great things the Lord has done for us!'

With the help of Walter Melotti, the businessman Arthur met on his first visit to Modena, they rented suitable quarters, consisting of four rooms on the second floor of an Italian home, with a private entrance. To their relief, the landlord and his wife lent the new couple furniture, since they had nothing but Shirley's bed. The man was retired and spent much of his time working in the yard and garden. They seemed very friendly, and the 'Italian grandma' was delighted to have a baby in the house. She offered to babysit Shirley when necessary. Their daughter and son-in-law, with a nine-year-old boy, lived with them.

The group of believers that Art and Erma had visited in Sassuolo prior to their moving to Modena welcomed them back warmly. There were twelve Christian families meeting in three cities, Sassuolo, Fiorano, and San Venanzio. They were brought to Christ by their leader, Ettore Barozzini who was saved in Cannes, France, through the ministry of Brethren Assembly people. Because of World War II, in 1942 all foreigners were put out of France. Ettore returned to his home near San Venanzio, Italy with a burden to share the

89

gospel with relatives and friends, and he had done a good job of it.

Of the three bits of advice G. Christian Weiss gave Arthur, he had fulfilled two: he got married, and he was beginning a work in a city untouched by any other testimony. The third was already falling into place, too. Although Modena had no church, Arthur and Erma felt a close bond developing with the nearby Christian group. These folks held at least three services in homes each week. The local train ran hourly, so travel back and forth from Modena was feasible. Since no one in the group was trained for the ministry, they were always pleased when Arthur would come to preach. On the other hand, he was encouraged and inspired by these devoted Christians who were so eager to learn more from the Word of God, and had such a desire to win others.

From the beginning it was clear that the ministry in Modena would be multifaceted. Modena was a center from which the arms of Christian leadership would reach out in many directions. Not the least of these was the ministry of encouragement and building up of the numerous groups of believers meeting in homes throughout the area and the small established churches, some without leaders. Art immediately set out to visit those he could reach by train. On his mind as he visited university towns was the love of his heart, the ministry of winning students to Christ and mentoring them. This could best be done through starting Intervarsity groups in the universities.

Planning and distribution of Christian literature would remain a priority ministry for Art. He walked the streets of Modena praying and searching for hearts hungry for the truth. His many business contacts, strangers on trains, and anyone he spoke to was offered a tract. The Bible had been a forbidden book for generations, so few Bibles could be

90

found. Frequently people asked for New Testaments. Arthur found a man at the market who had been looking for a source from which to purchase Bibles, because people kept asking for them. Art kept him supplied.

Erma's ministry with VBS and camps would continue, and she took children from Sassuolo to camp at Poggio Ubertini, where she and Maria Teresa had held camps each year. As soon as the 1953 summer camps were over, she started two small Sunday schools, one for believers' children held at Sassuolo (traveling to and from by train every Sunday morning) and Modena (in the afternoon). Her hospitality would be a vital part of the total outreach. And as time went on, her creative mind, organization skills, tireless service, and enthusiasm for every aspect of the ministry would touch all of Italy and beyond through camps, VBS, radio, and literature.

One of the first items of business on the agenda was to check in at the police headquarters to apply for permission to stay there indefinitely as missionaries. The Modena police were cordial, and since the Wiens' permission to stay in Florence as students was valid until July 31, they accepted that. Because they were new in Modena, the police granted them another six months. Art explained that their status had changed. They were no longer students, but were seeking permission to remain now as missionaries. Not to worry; when the six months was up police headquarters would write to Rome for permanent status. In less than six months, however, they received the first order to leave the country, and four similar orders shocked them and put everyone involved into a mode of unceasing, fervent prayer for the intervention of God.

In Modena, two families were willing to attend services in the Wiens home, a family whose son had urged them to come to Modena, and the Melotti family who had helped them in so many ways. The Melottis had attended a church in Bologna a few times. The Wiens hesitated to seem pushy, but to their delight the Melottis requested a Bible study in their home. A few months later during an invitation to dinner, Mrs. Melotti and her thirteen-year-old daughter Paula accepted Christ.

Art and Erma rented a piano and began a Sunday afternoon evangelistic meeting in their apartment. Inviting folks they met day-to-day in Modena became second nature. A few people came to the service several times, but the threats of the local priest intimidated many. People frequently expressed fear of attending anything that was not Catholic. Almost every week, Christians from Sassuolo came by train to encourage the Wiens, and several biked the sixteen kilometers. The first five months they had an average attendance of eighteen. Of those who came, forty-two who had dropped in a time or two were unsaved. This was the first evangelical service many of them had ever attended, so having such a good turnout was very encouraging.

The military school at Modena, the 'West Point' of Italy, beckoned Arthur, and he prayed for an entrance to witness there. His contact at a local army camp came at the market. As he was delivering Bibles to the merchant in the marketplace, two soldiers who had been following him stepped up. One was a Christian and the other seeking the truth. Arthur was pleased to learn that they were from cities where there were strong evangelical churches. He invited them to the Sunday afternoon evangelistic service, hoping they would grow in understanding and be able to help their home churches when they got out of the army.

From that small beginning, soldiers began coming to the Wiens home for the Sunday afternoon service. At least one evening a week they would drop in for an informal gathering. They loved to sing, so they spent time around the piano singing gospel hymns. It became customary then to read a chapter from the Bible and discuss it. During a prayer time, they encouraged Christian soldiers to pray aloud. If there was time, they ended the evening playing games, sometimes offering them a snack or a supper.

In a very short time, four soldiers who had never had contact with Christians before accepted Christ as their own personal Savior. Ivo, a young man from Genoa, went to work after high school but continued to read. When he came to Modena and heard about the Bible, he immediately determined to buy one. He read almost all of it in the three months he was stationed in Modena. Art described Antonio, one of the soldiers Ivo led to Christ, as 'sitting on the edge of his seat during meetings, drinking in every word'. Before Ivo left, he led two other soldiers to Christ.

Pietro, on the other hand, was a farm boy from Sicily who was illiterate. He began attending an army evening school so he could learn to read the Bible. When he was the only Christian soldier left in Modena Art and Erma wondered whether he would succeed in bringing someone else, but they prayed with him to that end every time he came. How thrilled he was when he found another boy from Sicily (also named Pietro – Peter) who would come along! They worked together at the army camp, so they talked about the gospel often. The second time he came, this boy also accepted Christ. One evening the doorbell rang and there were three soldiers. They had brought a third Sicilian lad, Antonio, who was familiar with the gospel.

Many of the soldiers came from large cities with good churches, but the two from Sicily went home to an area where there was no evangelical witness.

Art's entrance into the university in Modena came through a letter from a fellow missionary saying that a Greek student who had accepted Christ was transferring to Modena. He came to the first service they held in their home, and brought a friend. Thus the Sunday afternoon evangelistic service in the Wiens home kept reaching here and there, bringing new people under the hearing of the gospel.

The believers at Sassuolo had their own morning service in a home, so early every Sunday before church there, Erma held a Sunday school. Children's meetings were brand new to them, so Sunday school was popular and the children eagerly invited their friends. Stories, lessons, songs, memory work – everything was exciting to them.

One day Art and Erma visited in the home of a four-year-old Sunday school pupil. Little Olivia said to Erma, 'Look, American lady, I want to show you something.' Off she went to get a big old purse. She put its long handle around her neck, with the big purse hanging down in front of her. 'Now watch me unlatch it,' she said. She began to make the motions of playing an accordion, and she started singing a hymn from an open hymnbook before her (which of course she couldn't read).

Olivia and her brother brought another girl to Sunday school, a child of about twelve. She loved the activity the first Sunday, but then she dropped out. They said she was sent to a boarding school. She was apparently disciplined too harshly, so her father took her out, and to Erma's delight, she was back in Sunday school. She attended three weeks and was ever so interested. The following Sunday she was back again, declaring that she liked the Christian way and wanted to follow Christ. They felt she would soon be saved.

But in Italy Satan's victims are not so easily claimed. When she got home that day, an older girl visiting at the house tore up her Bible verses and gave her a fierce scolding. She threatened to slap her if she ever dared to return to Sunday school. The child played with the Christian children all week and insisted she would be there Sunday, but on Saturday the young lady returned. Whatever happened, the little girl never came back to play with her friends, and never returned to Sunday school.

A woman named Rosanna came to work for Erma, to help in the house. One Monday morning when she arrived she told Erma that her seven-year-old son had come home from Sunday school (in Modena) and talked to her about heaven and hell. Erma was cautious, wanting to be sure the woman was sincere. She said that if Rosanna wanted to learn more about heaven and hell, she should return in the afternoon and they would talk about it. She was sincere. She came back that afternoon, understood the gospel, and accepted Christ as her own personal Savior. From then on, she and Erma started their day with Bible reading and prayer.

One Sunday six young people from Florence came to spend the day with Art and Erma. They went along to Sassuolo, where on that Sunday Mr. Barozzini was conducting a baptismal service. It took a great deal of courage for anyone to take the public step of baptism in Italy, but seven people testified in this public manner that they were born again believers, following the evangelical way. Arthur spoke at the service that morning, and the presence of the young Christians from Florence was a special encouragement to the group. Their train back to Florence didn't leave until 11:21 p.m. (Yes, precisely 11:21), so after the afternoon evangelistic service in Modena, they spent a long evening in the Wiens home.

Luciano Petrucci was another visitor, not for a day, but for several days. After he received his doctorate in engineering, he was expected to fulfill his required year of military service. He was in limbo, waiting to be called up for the draft, so he came to Modena to see how he could help. He put his engineering knowledge to work systematizing the home, a seemingly endless job with three family members and an active stream of visitors in such a small space. Sunday afternoon he and Arthur went to Fiorano, where Luciano spoke on peace from John 14:6, and gave his testimony. As he told how he had been converted simply by reading the Word of God, a man in the group said that since the war he had been searching for a Bible, but never found one. He had come to the right place!

So many like him were searching for the truth. One by one God guided them to those who could help. As Arthur wrote, 'One must experience the joy of giving out the Word to one who has never heard it before to understand what a thrill that is!' At Fiorano, Sassuolo, San Venanzio, and other locations, they continued to give out the truths of the gospel, always to groups of believers hungry to understand the Bible better, and always to a few unsaved people in the crowd.

Suddenly, just when they thought everything was going so right, a dark cloud arose on the horizon. The owner of the home they lived in said they would have to move. They could no longer have services in his home. He first said it disturbed him and his neighbors. However, he had been called before the local priest who had threatened him because he was harboring the evangelicals. The priests were powerful, so such an experience was terrifying for the average Italian. With heavy hearts Art and Erma began searching for another house for themselves, praying that they would find one where they would be completely free to continue their ministry.

Nor was the situation concerning their residency permits

Cpl. Art Wiens, Chaplain's Assistant, with his jeep near the war front at Pistoia, Italy.

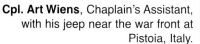

The Alfredo del Rosso family, who opened their home in Florence, Italy to servicemen during the war, and welcomed Art Wiens back to Italy in 1950.

Wedding day, Florence, 1951 *(L to R, Luciano Petrucci, Arthur and Erma Wiens, and Maria Teresa DeGiustina).*

First-term missionaries with their baby Shirley, 1953, preparing to leave their Christian friends in Florence to begin a pioneer work alone in Modena.

Erma and Shirley with their first car, 1954.

Erma's first Sunday school class at Sassuoulo.

Whenever he could, Arthur began home Bible studies to win and disciple people he met.

Erma Wiens recording her verbal translation of Danny Orlis stories.

Valeria Brenton putting Erma's translation into smooth-flowing, literary Italian.

Pioneer radio: Erma Wiens and Samuele Negri reading Danny Orlis for Erma's youth program.

Professor Gianunzio Artini, beloved Italian evangelist, chosen by Back to the Bible Broadcast to begin adult radio broadcasts.

Ascoltate

Voce della Bibbia

Arthur in the Voce della Bibbia booth at Modena's large trade fair.

David Hansen, now International Director of Back to the Bible Broadcast, as a Voce della Bibbia technician, 1978.

Mario Pieri, a technician at Voce della Bibbia, with Gloria and their children, John and Matteo.

Voce della Bibbia staff in the 1980s.

Shirley *(L)* **and Gloria Wiens** ready to be baptized in a river.

Claudio and Shirley Simonini's children in 1989 *(L to R, Laura, Stefano, Cristina, and Simona).*

After college, Gloria works with her mother in the CEM office opened in in Modena in 1985, preparing the Scripture Calendar.

Erma Wiens surrounded by students in her evening Bible School.

The CEM bookstore just off a main street (L to R, Mrs. Angus Hudson, wife of key British publisher, with Daniel, Erma and Arthur Wiens).

Il Traguardo staff on its 20th anniversary (L to R, Alberto, Arthur, Erma, Rossana Marinelli, Shirley Wiens, Betty Jabs and Gloria Wiens).

"Aunt Betty," homemaker for the Wiens family, cared for Erma's youngest child, Danny, becoming almost a second mother to him.

Daniel Wiens leaving Italy for Black Forest Academy in Germany.

Arthur and Erma Wiens.

settled. They were told that a survey was done showing that there were not enough evangelicals in the district to warrant having a missionary there. Another letter was sent to the Ministry of the Interior at Rome by the Modena police headquarters requesting indefinite stay for the Wiens in Italy. The only reply was that they needed more information about their mission board and its scope in Italy. The mission contacted the State Department in Washington; they suggested Art and Erma present their case directly to the man at the American Embassy in Rome who handled such matters.

On the plus side, the trip to Rome allowed them to visit scattered groups of believers in need of encouragement, and to see friends, ministering along the way. The official at the Embassy recommended that Arthur put through another request for permission to stay (even though he had been told he could not); the official promised to take it directly to the Italian government and to speak on their behalf. Since their closest church connection was Brethren, the new request was to be accompanied by a letter from the administrative president of the Open Brethren Church in Italy requesting their presence so that they could continue to offer spiritual help to the scattered groups of believers near Modena.

Meanwhile, letters criss-crossed the ocean from Arthur to Dr. Clyde Taylor, who represented evangelical interests in Washington, D.C., and from the State Department to the American Embassy in Rome. The request had been narrowed down to permission to stay one more year, until December 1955 when their furlough was due. Staff at the police headquarters in Modena became friendly, even to accepting New Testaments from Arthur, who was almost a fixture there. They joked that they just couldn't get him out of the country! Arthur was firm that God had sent him to Italy, and he intended to stay. Some replies from Rome, transmitted by the police, were fearfully plain.

Dec. 16: Called to the police department and shown a telegram that they had to be out by Dec. 31, 1953.

Dec. 17: Arthur to Rome, but given little hope that they would be allowed to stay.

Dec. 18: Another telegram from Rome. They had to leave by Dec. 31.

Dec. 20-25: A week of visiting homes and preparing to leave.

Dec. 26: A reprieve; a letter from Washington saying not to move until they received instructions from American Embassy.

Dec. 27: Called Rome; there was to be a conference with the Italian government concerning their case and others. Told to inform the police of this, and request permission to stay awaiting results. Police said, 'No! – Dec. 31 out!' If they didn't go willingly, riot police would escort them to Genoa, and they would be put out of the country.

Dec. 28: Embarrassing for the police department; a telegram from Rome saying the American missionaries could stay.

Dec. 29: A thanksgiving and praise service at Sassuolo!

Just when they gave up finding a one-family home, or any home better suited to their needs, the owner of their present apartment relented. He said they could stay, but he asked that they have only small gatherings. Since many of those attending the evangelistic services were from Sassuolo, they decided to discontinue the Sunday afternoon meeting in Modena. They would hold small Bible studies in their home or the homes of others, praying for a group large enough to eventually rent a room that would be suitable for meetings.

Meanwhile, they and any who wished to go along would worship with the folks in the homes around Sassuolo.

During this and other stressful periods in their lives, Art and Erma tended to encourage one another. Erma's faith seemed to grow stronger in tough times. Sometimes she would remind Art of his Victorious Living class at Columbia Bible College, a class that had been so helpful to him. She would suggest he reread some of the notes and the scripture that accompanied them. Victorious living meant soaring above the storms, holding on and trusting when no other course of action was possible. They would talk about these things, and pray for one another. When the very foundations of their ministry seemed ready to crumble, such exercises in faith strengthened them.

In April 1954, the Lord gave them their first car. Arthur, often accompanied by believers, increased his visits to remote villages to distribute literature and encourage isolated groups of Christians. In September, he and Giorgio, a young believer from Sassuolo, held a VBS in Fontanelle, 50 kilometers from Modena. Each evening they held evangelistic meetings. Erma, with four young Italian Christians, held several Vacation Bible Schools at villages near the Adriatic sea in southern Italy. In every way, the car broadened the ministry and brought virtually inaccessible locations within their reach.

A year after they had been present for a baptism for seven believers at Sassuolo, another baptismal service was held for four men. Enzo, a husky young man of twenty-three, was from a Christian home. He first came with a friend, but the other boy's parents objected and said they would rather he die than have their son evangelical. Despite his friend's turning back, Enzo continued, and was now ready for baptism.

A farmer, thirty-two, attended the special service at Sassuolo when Art and Erma first visited from Florence. He was impressed with the gospel, but was afraid to be seen attending services near his home. When he learned that services were being held at the Wiens home in Modena, he went there. After several months, one evening in their home he accepted Christ. Shortly after that his courage increased and he attended first at Sassuolo, and finally in his home town, Fiorano. He was a member of the Communist party, but neither that nor his inherited Catholic religion brought him the peace for which he longed, and which he found in following Christ.

The third man was older, a man from the factory in Sassuolo where there were already four Christians. First he accepted a tract; then he asked to borrow a Bible so he could read it for himself. After several weeks he began attending Fiorano services. The first service he attended he stayed until after midnight asking questions about the Bible. When the way of salvation was made clear to him, he gladly accepted Christ as his Savior.

The fourth man, Celeste, first came to the services as a spy, to gain information to use against the evangelicals. However, the message touched his heart, and he returned later to a meeting for the right reason, to find out more about the gospel. He cut off connections with his political party and became a faithful follower of Christ. His family often called the priest in to their home to try to persuade Celeste to return to the Roman Catholic Church. He remarked that when he was out in the world and deep in sin they didn't care, but when he became a child of God they were upset, as if he had done something terribly wrong.

A month after the baptismal service, Arthur arrived home from a trip to find that Celeste, only thirty-seven, had died from a blood clot on the brain. Although he survived three days, he never regained consciousness. The family began arranging with the priest for burial, but Christian brothers stepped in and suggested that Celeste would have preferred a Christian burial. Very reluctantly, someone from the family went to the priest and got permission for an evangelical funeral, the first in Sassuolo. Permission had to be obtained from the mayor and from the chief of the police, as well.

Over three hundred people gathered in front of the home for the memorial service, and even more went to the cemetery. Two of the young men baptized with Celeste stood at the gate of the cemetery handing out tracts, and those who attended heard an Italian brother give the way of salvation very clearly as Celeste was laid to rest. Although his life as a believer was very short, his testimony through death was powerful.

In November 1954, Sunday services resumed in Modena at a rented room large enough for public meetings and an office. The owner drew up and signed a contract stating that the room could be used for evangelical services. The Sunday afternoon services were attended by about eighteen, a Thursday night Bible study by a few less. Erma also resumed her Modena Sunday school at the new rented room.

The year granted them to stay was a busy, happy, successful year, filled with opportunities in all areas of their ministry as God poured out his blessings on the region of Emilia. One of their last efforts was to mail 9,000 tracts to homes in their area. An average of 50 responses a month came, requesting New Testaments. Some people also wanted to enroll in the correspondence courses. Many people heard the gospel for the first time, some of them in the new rented hall in Modena. The torch of God had weathered a very bad storm, but it was still shining brightly. God had brought them through it all safely. They had known they could trust Him; He had proved himself to them, and to the countless number of Italian Christians who prayed with them and watched the drama from beginning to end.

At 6:00 p.m. November 28, 1955, they left Modena by train for a year's furlough in Canada and the U.S. The farewell at Modena was the hardest parting either Art or Erma had ever experienced in their lives. At the station were several whom they had led to the Lord, others who had been Christians when they arrived, but had been led into a life of victory through the teaching of the Word, and by their example. Many were crying as they prayed for each other. The train pulled away, leaving the tearful crowd on the platform sadly waving goodbye. They arrived at Genoa at 10:00 p.m. and sailed for New York aboard the S.S. *Andrea Doria*, December 1, 1955.

The initial joy of visiting family and friends had barely subsided when they were hit with a new crunch of uncertainty. The year-long furlough stretched into two years, as the Italian government refused to grant visas for Art and Erma Wiens to return to Italy. At last, in April 1957, they received a 12th letter from Dr. Clyde Taylor in Washington which was very encouraging: 'The State Depart-ment called us and said they had referred your case to the Embassy in Rome, and the Embassy in Rome has casually mentioned your name to the Italian government to let them know that the Embassy is interested in your visa.'

In June, 'The Italian law now requires that missionaries coming to Italy must prove that their presence is necessary by a church or group of churches and that these churches are recognized before the Italian government.'

Again, God triumphed. Art and Erma Wiens, and Shirley, now five years old, sailed from New York to Genoa aboard the beautiful S.S. Independ-ence. They couldn't help but grin at each other frequently and reminisce, realizing that their return to Italy was nothing short of a miracle, God pulling rank on the devil.

Arthur held the Protestant service the two Sundays they were on board. The captain, some crew members, and quite a few passengers attended. Since the ship was scheduled to dock at Casablanca, they hoped to see missionary friends planning to be there when the ship came in. However, a storm made it impossible to enter that port. They moved on into the Mediterranean, where according to the ship's daily newspaper, the S.S. Independence rescued a British couple whose sloop had floundered in the storm.

Extra special events such as this rescue, and even normal events seemed very precious to the happy Wiens family. They were on their way back home to Modena – with permission to stay for three years!

Chapter 6

The Miracle of Radio!

When the Wiens family stepped onto Italian soil at Genoa a week before Christmas 1957, a settled feeling of joy and peace swept over them. Arthur was the first to greet old friends in Modena, because the customs office at the port required a certificate of residence before releasing the baggage. While Erma and Shirley waited in Genoa at the home of missionary friends, he took the first train to Modena and arrived at the Ferrari home in Fiorano at midnight, to an exuberant welcome. The next day, Primo Ferrari took Art to the mayor's office, where the necessary certificate was quickly supplied. Back in Genoa, the chief official at the port filled out the customs report without incident, and charged only 50 lire (8 cents). The baggage was shipped to Modena and finally, Art, Erma, and Shirley were on their way home.

The Ferraris, almost like family to Art and Erma, invited them to stay until they found a place to live. Since their home in Fiorano was only 150 feet from the largest shrine to Mary in the province of Modena, evangelical services there were held right in the path of pilgrims going to the shrine. Sometimes the group met at the Casolari farm home in the hills above Fiorano, a comfortable home with a huge open fireplace serving as kitchen stove. Services were still being held at Sassuolo, Fiorano, and San Venanzio, changing homes as the need required.

The Wiens arrived on Saturday night, so after the 'breaking of bread' on Sunday morning at Fiorano, Arthur preached. He chose Psalm 126:3, 'The Lord hath done great things for us, whereof we are very glad!' In the afternoon service at Sassuolo, he spoke from Acts 12, the account of Peter's deliverance from prison by an angel in answer to the church's prayers. After two years away, his Italian was rusty, but his audiences were forgiving. It felt so right to have the Wiens family back with them!

If only youth workers had a periscope to see beyond the years to the good results of their ministries! Giorgio Ferrari, a young man who was saved at age fifteen in the Sassuolo church, was developing into a solid Christian. When Art and Erma left, he was in his last year of school in Modena. Like other young people, he often came by the Wiens' home to hang out and to help. Art had asked Giorgio to send out the Testaments and correct the Bible correspondence course lessons while they were gone. It was a big responsibility to give such a young man, but they found that he had enlisted the help of his sister Nerina and had faithfully carried out the work. Giorgio also graduated from school with top honors.

While it was exciting to catch up on all the news, they were eager to get back into the ministry. The first step was to spend three months brushing up on the language. Febe Cavazzutti had married a doctor (her name was now Rossi), and had moved to Padua, a city of 170,000, ninety miles northeast of Modena, not far from Venice. Arrangements had been made through correspondence for Febe to tutor Art and Erma again, so in early January they left the Modena area to move to Padua.

Their new home was a small furnished apartment on the 13th floor, right in the middle of town. From their windows they could see much of the city, and when it was clear, even the snow covered Alps in the distance. Their church choice was easy – at least there *was* a Protestant church in Padua, one small Methodist church. Shirley started Kindergarten in a public school in Padua. Her teacher was a nun, and she had to learn to understand and speak fluent Italian.

Before furlough, Arthur had taken a group to evangelize Pavullo, a town in the Apennine Mountains about 40 miles above Modena. They distributed tracts in many of the small mountain villages in the area. Twenty-one people from Pavullo wrote in response to the tracts requesting New Testaments. This was a much higher return than usual, so although they could not go back, they had prayed regularly for the people of Pavullo.

As in so many cases, the Lord was at work in His quiet, miraculous ways, bringing the gospel to people whose hearts were ready to receive it. Many men left their homelands to find work, and some from Pavullo went to Belgium, where good money could be had in the mines. One of these men had been saved, and while he was back in Pavullo for a vacation, he told his friends and relatives about it. Some of them were converted, too. The priest of his village and even the archbishop of Modena tried unsuccessfully to hinder the testimony.

In a roundabout way, Art and Erma heard this story while they were in Canada and they were eager to see for themselves what the Lord had done and minister to the new believers they had heard about. In February 1958, when returning to Modena for a wedding, the Wiens stayed the weekend so they could visit Pavullo. They took four Christian young people along and held an evening meeting in a mountain home. In the fall, Arthur returned to hold several evening meetings. The opposition from the priests was fearsome, so only a few people attended. One who came was

106

an elderly man who, even when it rained, walked almost two hours to get there. Occasionally from that time on, they visited Mr. Manfredini's home when they could.

All the prayers for more workers in Italy and all the appeals for missionaries to join the work in Italy paid off. Each year there were new faces at the annual missionary conference. At last on June 5, 1958, Abe and Mary Unrau, from British Columbia, arrived to serve in the GMU work. Arthur was at Genoa to meet them. He found a place on the terrace of the port to watch as the big ship docked and the 400 passengers disembarked. He was amused at the emotional Italians greeting their loved ones, but when Art saw Abe and Mary and hurried toward them, his own emotions overflowed. He met them in a typical Italian embrace, with a kiss on each cheek! He helped them through customs and went to secure a residence permit.

Abe and Mary began their language study at Padua, living in the Wiens' apartment. Later they moved to Florence to study in the foreign language school at the university.

Shirley had undergone surgery to remove her adenoids. To improve her health, the doctor prescribed sea air, so they joined the crowds of vacationers camping at the beach for the month of June. Shirley's health did improve, plus they found a whole new audience for their witness. In August Erma was involved in Bible camps with Maria Teresa.

Finally in the fall, the Wiens were ready to settle back in Modena. Single family houses were almost nonexistent in the city. They rented a third floor apartment in a big old house owned by the Maranis. The attic was theirs for storage. Erma, with her creative talent, set to work turning it into a comfortable home. They brought some household goods back from America. They hired a carpenter to make oak furniture: a dining table and chairs, a corner cupboard, bookshelves. She wallpapered and made curtains and bedspreads.

Shirley developed asthma. This time the doctor recommended that to get away from the damp, foggy weather of Modena they should take her to the mountains. They chose Pavullo. There they met Erio, the miner from Belgium whose testimony started the ministry. He was home for a six-week vacation, so he often went with Arthur in his visitation and they attended services at Fiorano together. During that time Art visited everyone in the area who had written for New Testaments and made other new friends. This led to starting Tuesday evening Bible studies which rotated from home to home, including Mr. Manfredini's, which was an hour's walk from the car. In June 1959, Mr. Manfredini (76) was baptized at Fiorano with several others.

Several people mentioned to Arthur that they had never seen a Bible nor had they seen any evangelical books. He and his friend Ettore Barozzini, from Sassuolo, approached the mayor of Pavullo to request that his office display evangelical books to give the people opportunity to read them. The mayor gladly accepted the offer. Books such as 'On Being a Real Christian', 'Pilgrim's Progress', 'Livingston in Africa', and Ironside's 'Great Words of the Bible' were displayed on the main street by the librarian.

Gloria Ann Wiens was born on January 21, 1960, the baby sister Shirley had been hoping for! Erma had created a flouncy bassinet with ruffles and bows, where visitors wanting to see the baby girl often found her. They planned to dedicate her at Fiorano and invited many people, but they hesitated to invite the landlady, Mrs. Marani, who came up every day to see the new baby. She and her husband were staunch Catholics accustomed to baptisms in magnificent cathedrals. Gloria's dedication was to be held in a simple home. However, shortly before the day arrived, Shirley asked her if she was coming. 'If you want me to,' she replied. She came, along with her husband, daughter, and sister. They had no comments about their first evangelical service, except that the husband said he liked the prayers, 'from the heart, and not memorized'.

After completing their language study, Abe and Mary Unrau moved to Pavullo, the first resident missionaries in that area. Abe had accompanied Art Wiens on several witnessing trips to the region. As a very young girl in Canada Mary had begun witnessing to Catholics, even confronting a priest with the truth. Both Abe and Mary were well aware of the difficulties they would face. Still, it was unnerving to have the priest drive through the streets warning the townspeople over a loudspeaker that if any of them gave 'those foreign devils' a house to live in a host of curses would befall it.

The Unraus made many friends throughout the area, with excellent success in witnessing. In the ten years they were at Pavullo, their lives spoke as loudly as their words. They planted a strong church and made close friends all over the area. In addition to the daily witness through their home and church ministry, Abe was a tireless traveler with his Bible van, taking the gospel to fairs large and small, and reaching unreached areas through literature distribution and verbal witness. They still return to Italy frequently to visit the area , and Abe, a well-loved speaker, holds meetings elsewhere in the country when he comes.

Abe and Mary were joined in 1963 by Silvano and Liliana Casolari. Silvano's parents hosted the meetings at Fiorano, so like Giorgio and Nerina Ferrari, he attended the Evening Bible School and had been a willing helper in the Modena ministry, preparing and distributing literature and going on home visitation and holding home Bible studies with Arthur.

While in Switzerland, Silvano answered the call of God to serve Him full time. He met and married Liliana, a Swiss Christian who also wanted to serve the Lord. Liliana had learned Italian during a year in Italy and she had one year of training at Emmaus Bible Institute in Switzerland. After their marriage, Silvano and Liliana moved to Vignola, not far from Pavullo and worked along side the Unraus. Silvano got a license to sell Bibles in the markets, a very effective outreach.

Thus, one town after another was added to the missionaries' circuit. But in Modena, their target city, there still was no church. With the help of the young people, the Wiens sent out 19,000 letters to people listed in the Modena phone book. The mailing contained a tract, a coupon offering a free Gospel and a correspondence course, and a letter encouraging them to read the Bible.

The responses were gratifying. Many phoned, some very favorable, wanting only to inquire about the people who sent out the letter. It was easy to reply to them. A little more difficult were the calls from angry people, some displeased because the literature didn't carry the imprint of the Roman Catholic Church. Responses requesting the free Gospel of John and correspondence course poured in. Since Modena was the target area, getting acquainted with those interested was a special pleasure.

For his project in a Church Growth Principles class at Moody Bible Institute, Philip Schroeder, a GMU missionary to Italy, presented a very perceptive paper titled, 'Church Growth Survey of the Modena Churches in Northern Italy'. He divided the years of evangelical effort from World War II to the time of his writing, into three eras:

1946-1960: A time of direct opposition from the Roman Catholic Church. Freedom of Religion was constitutional, but not practiced. Italians were held bondage to the priests, and evangelical witness was not tolerated.

1961-1977: A time of maturing and church growth. In 1965 the Roman Catholic Council called Vatican II, which included the Ecumenical Council and Declaration of Religious Liberty. Hostility toward evangelicals decreased.

1977-1987: Years of 'boom and strife'. We will examine that later.

As in many countries, the only radio broadcasting in Italy was government controlled. For a brief time after World War II while the Allies were peacekeeping in Italy, the chaplains had succeeded in getting religious broadcasts on the air. They had not continued.

In 1959, Jack Murray started three radio broadcasts beamed into Italy from Radio Tangier, a small short-wave station on the northern coast of Morocco. In 1960, Jack spent several days in Modena following up his radio contacts. He and Arthur also went to Rome to meet with Clarence Jones of HCJB, Quito, Ecuador, whose powerful station reached many countries of the world. Jones was meeting with people in Italy interested in missionary radio. He announced plans to purchase time on a powerful secular radio station in Europe to air evangelical programs.

This news was exciting to Erma. Her love for children and youth had encompassed large groups through VBS and summer camps, some in areas far from Modena. Her mind was always on those who were not being reached, and she longed to contact them. There was also the problem of persecution. Italians young and old were kept from attending evangelical functions by fearful or fanatical family members. Radio would most certainly give youth an opportunity to listen to the Word in secret, if necessary. What great possibilities! Her mind ran full speed ahead, and her prayers tried to reign it in to seek the Lord's will!

In 1961, as the fresh breezes of religious freedom began to flow across northern Italy, Richard Wolff of Back to the Bible Broadcast, Lincoln, Nebraska, came to visit Art and Erma Wiens. With them was the Back to the Bible representatives from Marseille, France. Back to the Bible was broadcasting Richard Wolff's messages in French from the new Trans World Radio in Monte Carlo. Over the first three years they had forwarded names of eighty Italian listeners to the French broadcast to Art and Erma for follow-up.

To expand the witness in Italian, Gian Nunzio Artini, a well-loved Italian evangelist, was to prepare one 15-minute adult broadcast a week. Wolff invited Erma Wiens to do a children's broadcast in Italian. Arthur was to be director of the Italian branch of the Back to the Bible office to be set up in Modena under the name *Voce della Bibbia,* Voice of the Bible.

The Wiens made a quick trip to Marseille, France for orientation at the Back to the Bible Broadcast branch there, to learn how to set up an office in Modena. For one year they worked out of their home, finally renting a small apartment for the office. This was pioneer radio, so recording of the first broadcasts was done in a rather primitive manner. Bob Jones, a missionary at Florence, had brought excellent radio equipment back after furlough. They produced the first broadcasts in the studio set up in his home. The first four children's broadcasts were recorded in Florence August 31 and September 1, and on September 5 (the Wiens' 10th wedding anniversary), Art and Erma returned to Florence for the recording of Professor Artini's first four adult broadcasts.

The first broadcasts were to be aired October 7th and 8th, Mr. Artini's on Saturday at 1:15 p.m. (Italian time) and Erma's program every Sunday at 1:30 p.m. Shirley, in the fourth grade now at the Italian school, announced the news of her mother's broadcasts to her thirty-five classmates, urging them to tune in.

Twenty-seven adults wrote to the new office during the first two months of broadcasting. The first letter as a result of the adult broadcast was from a ham operator in Modena, who requested the book offering of the month, 'On Being a Real Christian', by G. Christian Weiss. The second month's book was Billy Graham's 'Peace with God'. As to the children's broadcasts, fifty-three children wrote in during the first eight broadcasts, from every area of Italy.

Annual fairs were held each year throughout Italy. Arthur always requested permission to have a booth at the Modena fair, but he was turned down. Instead for three years he took a group of young people to distribute tracts and talk to individuals at the gate, as they came or left the fair.

In 1962 he was finally granted permission for the booth he had prayed for so long. They would be allowed to give out literature and sell religious books and Bibles at the fair which ran from April 15-25, 1962. Despite a surprise spring snowstorm, they worked all day April 14 preparing the booth. For the background they had a large sign announcing *Voce della Bibbia*. On one side of the counter there was a tract rack with about fifty different tracts. A display of evangelical books and scripture wall mottos filled the rest of the booth. A large sign offered the entire Bible for only 1000 lire ($1.60 at that time). The booth was ideally located near the entrance to the fairground, so most of the 110,000 people couldn't help but see it. At midnight April 14, they were putting the final touches on the 10' x 10' booth.

Although the Catholic church didn't encourage people to read the Bible, the Catholic version was no longer prohibited. Just before the fair a major Italian publishing house began advertising weekly spots giving a simple summary of the Bible. It was an impressive advertising campaign, with announcements on radio and television, wall posters, and large signs at all the news stands. With the fear lifted, many people dared to come to the *Voce della Bibbia* booth and hold a Bible in their hands for the first time. Sales were excellent, and *Voce della Bibbia* received superb publicity at the fair.

Every effort was made to advertise the broadcasts. The Modena office sent letters to 800 Protestant churches and groups encouraging believers to invite their unsaved friends to listen. At the same time Arthur was working with a lawyer to legally incorporate *Voce della Bibbia* and Gospel Missionary Union. Legal status was granted to both.

There were some jobs that could be done by a volunteer group of young people, such as preparing the large mailings. It was clear, though, that a staff of permanent workers would be needed for the Voice of the Bible office. Even before the broadcasts began, Erma gave Nerina Ferrari a typing book and showed her how to teach herself to type. She did well and got a job, but after the broadcasts began, she felt led of the Lord to quit and come to work for Back to the Bible. Nerina was also sent to Marseille to learn how the records were kept, how the mailing lists were set up, and other general office procedures.

Her job at the Voice of the Bible office was the culmination of several years of growing in the Lord. Nerina was saved as a teenager in 1949, a very difficult time for an Italian young person to become a Christian. The persecution was unrelenting. The schools were public, not parochial. Just the same, she recalls, 'When we asked to be excused from religion classes, we were treated like scum,' Nerina adds, 'Evangelical students were not treated fairly in public schools.'

Christian young people were scattered in various towns, so they faced the ridicule standing alone or as a small minority. The elder of their church, Ettore Barozzini tried to encourage the Christian youth by saying, 'If they call you nasty names, you are blessed of God!' This was true, of course. He based it on Matthew 5:11-12. Nerina did not feel blessed during those humiliating times. Not until she was much older did she grasp the true meaning of those strange and unwelcome words.

Nerina found it too hard to live a Christian life. For three years she strayed, resentful and not willing to face the persecution. She decided the church rules were too strict. She writes, 'My whole attitude changed when in 1953, Arthur and Erma Wiens arrived with their beautiful little girl.'

During the time the Wiens were attending the Sassuolo group of meetings, the young people took notice of the new young Americans. They were radiant and enthusiastic Christians. When the Wiens started services in Modena, Giorgio and Nerina Ferrari were among those who attended. Flannelgraph 'images' had been considered evil, but Erma used them to teach her Sunday school lessons. This captured Nerina's attention and she began to learn the Word of God. 'Erma had a way of keeping us all interested and active,' she recalls. 'I didn't have time to go dancing!' Nerina was among the young people who attended the Evening Bible School at the Wiens home.

The Lord had picked an excellent person for the Voice of the Bible office. Nerina worked tirelessly, even helping in rush jobs by working with Art and Erma until midnight, if need be, to get finished. She learned to pray about everything, and was overjoyed when she saw definite answers to prayer. Conversions reported were precious to her. As new workers came, Nerina trained them, and helped keep the office work flowing smoothly through her efficient organization skills.

A year after the broadcast office was opened, October 14, 1962, the small group of believers in Modena moved into a rented hall for worship. For months the 'For Rent' sign had been in the window on the ground floor of the building where the *Voce della Bibbia* office was located. Several thought that it would be a good meeting place. Arthur called the owner and explained their need for a hall, and the owner had no objection to its being used for evangelical services.

Since the meeting hall was on a main street where many people passed by, a window display was prepared with the open Bible where it could be read. The attractive display was changed periodically. Sixty people attended the first Sunday service, including a photographer from the newspaper. It was the first Gospel service he had ever attended. He returned the following Sunday, not on assignment for the newspaper, but because he was personally interested in the gospel. Sunday school followed the morning worship service, not only for children, but including an adult class, rare in Italy.

Jean Padilla, who first ministered among Europeans in Morocco, had transferred to the French radio broadcast in Marseille. Before entering the Lord's work, he had been a carpenter, so he came to Modena to build furniture suited to the needs of the office: cabinets for the address files, literature storage, and other shelves and cupboards – even a pulpit for the new meeting hall. Padilla, an outgoing and godly man, encouraged everyone in the new work. While in Italy for the carpentry, he preached in the Modena area, as well as Bologna, Florence, and Genoa.

Erma had a gift for languages. She not only learned Italian quickly, but spoke fluently and generally without flaw. However, she determined that in a ministry as broad and important as radio, she needed the best editors available to check her work before recording it. Again reaching back into the past, she enlisted the help of Samuele and Vittoria Negri, who were already vital colleagues in translation and correspondence.

Vittoria, the daughter of a Florence family, attended the first girls' Bible camp directed by Erma and Maria Teresa at Poggio Ubertini. Vittoria was saved in 1951. Ten years later, she received her doctorate in literature. Her husband, Samuele, was from a Brethren family in northern Italy. Art and Erma met him at the Brethren young people's camp in 1951, and they were present when Samuele dedicated his life to serve the Lord. He studied three years at Emmaus Bible Institute in Switzerland. After their marriage Samuele and Vittoria moved to Rimini, about 100 miles from Modena, to begin a new work in that seacoast city. It was a drive both the Negris and the Wiens as co-workers would travel often!

One of the leaders of the new church was Remo Dosi, the new counselor at the Voice of the Bible office. Remo was born into a Christian home in Piacenza. In his late teens he had more interest in bicycle racing than in the gospel. His parents tried to keep him attending church, but it was not easy. He reluctantly agreed to go to evangelistic meetings for their sakes, but he sat in the back row and put his head behind the coats on the wall.

The evangelist was a fiery speaker, and before long, Remo found himself listening. He came out for the Lord that week, to the joy of his parents. Remo grew up in the church and attended the Brethren young people's camps for more than ten years. While at camp, he recorded the messages of Dr. Rene Pache and other inspiring youth speakers. During the long winter evenings he listened to these studies, so his doctrine and spiritual insight were excellent.

Voce della Bibbia was getting many letters with comments and questions that required the answers of a skilled counselor. Arthur felt that this ministry was not his gift; Erma didn't have time; Artini and Samuele lived out of town and neither of them had time. They all knew the Dosi family well enough to invite themselves to dinner, so one day the three men drove to Piacenza to meet with Remo. The family was honored to have these distinguished guests, but they had no idea why they had come.

At the dinner table, Professor Artini explained their need of a counselor at Modena. Remo wondered how he could fit in, but he immediately decided to come for a week to try it out. The week went well, and soon he moved his wife and family, three little girls and a boy, to Modena. His responses to listeners' letters were excellent and with the help of a good secretary to polish the grammar and spelling, he became a long-term, valued member of the staff.

Art and Erma's furlough was due in December 1962, but they chose to let Shirley complete the school year, leaving in June 1963. Erma did double duty on broadcast preparation, getting programs ready to cover the six months they would be gone. They left Remo and Nerina in charge during their furlough. Under the direction of Samuele Negri, and with the volunteers as needed, the work of the *Voce della Bibbia* office went smoothly without them.

Chapter 7

Aunt Betty Joins the Team

As all aspects of the ministry exploded at once, Erma became one busy lady. Gloria, a toddler whose chief talent was still her smile, loved being with her daddy. He took her with him whenever he could. However, he too was busy. His follow-up ministries ballooned, often requiring extensive travel. New administrative duties took time, thought and prayer. Both Art and Erma were involved in one area or another of literature production. Art often dealt with the printers, sometimes as far away as Naples. The Evening Bible School, local visitation, and various home Bible studies continued.

In addition to the time it took to prepare her programs, Erma checked her work with Vittoria Negri, sometimes in Modena, but often at the Negri home in Rimini. She went to Florence once each month for the recording. She was never idle when she traveled. She spent the time praying, reading, or working with the typewriter in her lap.

Phil Schroeder's wife, Sylvia, recalls a conversation with Erma that reveals at least in part the source of her strength. Sylvia was reading a current bestseller, and mentioned it to Erma. 'I read a fiction book once,' she said, 'and I didn't like the way it occupied my thoughts. I was so taken up by the book that I decided that I didn't want anything but the Lord to occupy my mind that much. That's why I try to read books that stimulate my thoughts to focus on the Lord.'

119

Sylvia comments, 'Her emphasis in life was to develop "the mind of Christ" in herself and to inspire others to focus their thoughts on Him. She weighed the value of things by their help or hindrance to her spiritual walk. Her conscious discipline of her mind was a great example to me.'

Erma, like Arthur, was a true workaholic. Her staff at the Back to the Bible office teased her that she wore them out, expecting them to work as hard as she did. Although she was authoritative, her personality was winsome and she immediately drew young people into her embrace. Her presence, filled with the joy of the Lord, could turn even tedious work projects into pleasure and learning sessions into merriment. Her staff respected and loved her, and willingly worked far beyond closing time when it was necessary to do so.

When a late-night job was completed, the volunteer work crew was treated to Erma's big homemade pizza, and on occasion, American cinnamon rolls, a favorite of the young people. Whether it was the relief at having a job completed, or just plain exhaustion, Erma became a different person late at night, laughing, giggling, having a wonderful time. Everyone joined in to the lighthearted banter as they stuffed themselves with their reward.

But to get it all done in the Lord's strength and not wear herself out by trying to do it through her own ingenuity, required sincere spiritual discipline. She prayed for the strength of the Lord, and she pressed forward in that strength.

Erma's diary of the years before the Wiens' second furlough has been preserved, and gives a touching picture of the life of a busy missionary mother, combining home and ministry. She mixes bread before going to the office, and serves fresh dinner rolls with the meal, because her family loves them. She helps Shirley with her homework (in Italian) and reads to her children (in English).

She does the laundry before going to the office. She cleans up the house and does some mending before going to the office. Before Sunday school she puts a turkey roll in the oven and prepares other things for company dinner. She teaches a children's class using flannelgraph, the Old Testament to young adults at the Evening Bible School, and fellowships with the students at Intervarsity meetings. She writes personal letters. She entertains overnight guests. She babysits for a staff member moving to town, and takes a meal to their home when the day is done.

She records the scripture she has read each day and what it meant to her. And at bedtime, she looks at her two sleeping children and writes, 'How blessed I am to have my two girls! They are so precious! My heart overflows with joy!'

Missionary children (or MKs, as they are affectionately called) grow up with unique and wonderful opportunities. They travel extensively. Shirley was a seasoned traveler in Europe. She made friends easily, loved being dropped off at Bible camps in Greece, England, Canada, and California, not intimidated by a whole new gang of kids. By the time she was four, Gloria had traveled to several European countries, Canada, and across the U.S. Long before foreign tourism was common, both girls traveled extensively. At fourteen, Shirley flew to Italy without her parents in order to get back in time for the opening of school.

Shirley and Gloria, born in Italy, were raised as Italians, but they spoke both languages and understood both cultures. They grew up helping in the ministry. Shirley was an enthusiastic witness and took part in evangelistic outreach as well as all other activities with the Italian young people. Both girls helped their mother on the broadcast. Shirley read stories to the children, at ease talking into the microphone.

Gloria's first experience was to sing 'Away in a Manger' on a Christmas broadcast.

Erma was an expert at controlling large groups of children and she ran a tight ship at home. It is probably typical to raise one's firstborn with a firm hand. She expected adult responses of Shirley – an only child for ten years. Shirley had little time to just be a kid. Things were easier for Gloria. A busy, working Mom eased up on the discipline. Gloria, who loved to be cuddled, has happy memories of spontaneous hugs and bedtime snuggling.

With the beginning of the broadcasts, the frenzied pace of constant deadlines had its price. The children, left with this care-taker and that, became emotional orphans. Their mom and dad were preoccupied with ministry, and it didn't help that the girls understood the importance of their mission. Parental 'quality time' was always squeezed in between more pressing matters.

Art and Erma went on their second furlough with a big burden, and everywhere they spoke, they mentioned this special request. They were praying for God to call someone to be their co-worker in Italy, to keep their household running smoothly and to give their children the stability of consistent loving attention even when they had to be gone. Someone was needed to see to the details of their children's lives, details they both knew all too well were getting lost in the crunch of their crowded schedules.

The first time they spoke to Erma's home congregation upon arrival in Ponoka, they mentioned this desire. No takers. While they went on deputation, Shirley stayed with Arthur's parents in California, where she attended school for four months. Although they presented the appeal for a co-worker over and over to various churches and conferences, no one responded. After six months of speaking

122

engagements, they went back to Erma's home church.

'Surely God has someone for this ministry,' they lamented to Erma's pastor. 'If people only understood how important this position is! How can we make the most of the enormous opportunities to win others in Italy, if we neglect the needs of our own girls?'

The pastor had been praying with them regarding this need. He had in mind a widow in the congregation. 'Why don't you go see Betty Jabs?' he suggested.

'I doubt that she would be interested,' replied Erma.

Betty Jabs was interested. Since their first visit she had prayed earnestly that the Lord would raise up someone to help them. It never occurred to her that she would be the one chosen by God in answer to her own prayer!

Betty was born in England, where, during World War II she met a Canadian soldier. In 1947 she left her homeland, moved to Canada, and married him. They settled in Ponoka in 1952, purchasing a small place on the outskirts of town. Betty bought a few laying hens from her neighbors, an elderly couple who in turn invited her to church. This resulted in her salvation, and her whole life was changed. A year later during evangelistic meetings, her husband too received Christ as his Savior. When her husband died suddenly in 1963, she was left completely alone, childless, her family far away in England. She called on the Lord in her distress, and He comforted her. She had a good job and a Sunday school class, and before long she was adjusting to her new life as a widow.

The pastor assured the Wiens that if Betty was the one for the job, the Lord would reveal it to her.

For three days after Art and Erma approached her, Betty Jabs struggled to make a decision. More than anything, she wanted to do the Lord's will. Art and Erma went back to

Modena in January 1964 rejoicing in answered prayer. 'Aunt Betty' was going to join their family! She arrived in Italy in March 1964.

Betty quickly discovered that this was no ordinary household. The Wiens home was something like a small hotel. No sooner had the guests departed and the beds were changed, in a few days other guests would be at the door. She saw that Arthur and Erma's home was really the headquarters for GMU, Back to the Bible Broadcast in Italy, and *Voce della Bibbia*, headquarters for Italian workers in radio and literature. In addition to guests connected with these ministries, many missionary friends came through.

Betty needed no coaxing to jump in and help. She could see that she was sorely needed. She was soon serving the Lord by cooking for the family and many, many guests, keeping house, and helping Erma with the immense laundry. The menial chores became easy as she accepted her role. She soon felt completely at home. It didn't take long for a sister relationship to develop as she and Erma fell into step, each one helping the other to keep the household running smoothly. Best of all, her mother heart reached out to embrace Gloria and Shirley. It was a perfect match. They soaked up her love and she soaked up theirs.

As a member of the Wiens household, Betty soon saw who was the 'handyman' of the family. Erma's floor polisher broke down, so she took it apart and discovered that the little steel friction brushes had worn out. She wrote her sister in Calgary for replacements. Ruth airmailed new ones to her, and when the replacement brushes arrived, Erma installed them. Betty says, 'Trust Erma to figure that out!' Since hiring an electrician was too expensive, a man in the church showed her how to do simple electrical wiring. She could install a new chandelier, or handle any other electrical job that came up.

124

Sometimes the two women worked side by side in the kitchen, tackling big jobs together. When Erma had a break at work and wanted to cook, bake, or squeeze in some sewing, Betty went to the office, where she worked in the mailing department. Betty was as versatile as Erma. She always said, 'I'm willing to do anything, type a letter or scrub the floors!' Most often, she was the stay-at-home caregiver. Shirley was eleven when she arrived, and Gloria, four. Aunt Betty had a life of her own, sharing an apartment with an Italian girl who worked in the office. This arrangement gave both her and her adopted family some private life.

Aunt Betty had followed the experiences of the Wiens family in prayer letters and through reports at her home church in Ponoka. She was aware that during the summer the doctors had recommended that Shirley be taken to the sea for at least two weeks, and if possible, a week or two in the mountains. The doctors believed that the long humid winters left the lungs in a weakened condition, and the sea air would strengthen them. The first summer Betty was with the Wiens family, she got to experience what camping was all about.

Mrs. Marani loved to watch from a shady spot in her yard as the Wiens family began to load up for camp. Perspiring and panting, they hauled their tent and other gear from the attic to their car, their loads of bedding, utensils, and food. When they returned from the sea, she watched the circus again as they took everything out and hauled it back up to the attic.

After setting up the tent and arranging things at the camp grounds, Arthur and Erma went back to Modena and their busy schedules and deadlines. Betty was left with Shirley and Gloria at the tent. She describes camp life as, 'fetching water from the cold water tap for cooking and drinking, and washing clothes by hand'. Shirley made friends with others of her age and didn't want Gloria always under foot, so Aunt Betty entertained Gloria while keeping the camp in order, washing clothes, making meals from scratch and cooking in the most primitive manner.

One day Gloria got very sick, so Betty asked Shirley to run to the camp director's office and ask him to get a doctor to come and see her. Betty knew no Italian at that time, so when the doctor came, Shirley had to translate. There was a virus in the camp, and many of the kids had come down with it. The doctor ordered medicine for Shirley to get at the nearby pharmacy, and Gloria got well.

Betty blended in at the office and saw the eternal value of all the hard work the staff was doing. She joined them in the staff prayer meetings, developing a love for radio listeners whose trials and joys she could help to share. The Lord gave the office staff, led by Remo Dosi and Nerina Ferrari, sensitivity as they sifted through the daily mail. As counselor, Remo composed the letters and answered the questions, but everyone in the office seemed to develop a gift for follow-up and shared the burden of keeping in touch with anyone who wrote. If someone requested a correspondence course, but didn't send in the first lesson, the name was put on a list for a follow-up letter. If they stopped the lessons halfway through, they received a letter. Thus, adults and children dawdling or close to dropping out were sometimes coaxed along by friendly letters.

In October the Evening Bible School reopened for the 1964-65 sessions. They met in the Wiens home Saturday nights, this time with ten students: Giorgio, Franca, Giuseppe, Valeria, Walter, Ellero, Franco, Daniela, and Shirley. Shirley, in the seventh grade, was studying Latin along with her other courses in school. She loved to study, and kept up with the older Evening Bible School students.

126

(Note: It may help to know that Franca is the feminine form of Frances; Franco is the male form, Francis. The 'a' or 'o' at the end of a name indicates if the person is male or female.)

Walter was an average Italian boy – as a child, religious, as a teenager, rebellious. Because he was active and aggressive, his rowdy ambition was soon channeled into the political activity of the communist party. One morning as he left for work at the sausage factory, Walter's attention was drawn to a slip of paper in the driveway. He jumped off his bike to pick it up.

What he found was a coupon advertising correspondence courses in the Gospel of John. Missionaries tossed Gospel tracts and coupons from their car windows as they drove through the streets. Some were lost, swept up by the street sweepers who didn't realize their value. Others were picked up and found much later in a pocket, a drawer, or even a wastebasket. Walter was curious about his, so he made contact with the missionaries and before long was saved. Walter, a young man from Formigine, began bringing his friend Ellero to regular meetings at Modena, their hometown church at Formigine, and a nearby town named Castelfranco, where meetings had been started. During eight years in a Roman Catholic school Ellero sought spiritual help, but he did not find it in religion. He found what he was looking for in Christ, and his testimony spoke to many at his baptism in Modena.

In the service on the Sunday of the baptism was an ex-priest who was saved as a result of the radio ministry. Now a school teacher, he learned of the broadcast from the first announcement the Wiens put in a magazine in 1961. For years he had been searching for spiritual help, and through the broadcasts he found peace in Christ.

In the Evening Bible School, Erma taught Bible Survey,

127

fascinating to those in the group who had not attended Sunday school, to whom the material was new. Remo Dosi taught Church History from the Protestant viewpoint, an eye-opener to the newer converts.

Arthur taught Personal Evangelism, with a special challenge for each student to begin praying for one individual they would like to win to the Lord. Most of them had gone with him at one time or another to distribute tracts and coupons, to follow-up contacts in the area, or to home Bible studies. He saw to it that all of his students had ample experience in outreach.

In November, when the universities opened, the Intervarsity group began meeting in the Wiens home once again. Students were drawn from the University of Bologna, as well as the Modena University. Among them, there were five who were able leaders for the study of Luke, which they had begun the previous year. Paula Melotti was working on her doctorate in Biological Sciences. Her family was the first in Modena to befriend the Wiens. She became the first person in Modena to accept the Lord. Now, almost fifteen years later, she became an active Christian. Paula came regularly and often led the meetings.

Sergio, who attended quite regularly, met Arthur on the street one day and told him that his mother's serious illness, got him to thinking of eternity. Another person who always attended had come into contact with liberal theology. It seemed to confuse and hinder him.

Cults had begun to move in at a rapid pace. Communism remained the strongest political force in Modena, so many people contacted claimed to be atheists. Even among the strongest of the Communists, the missionaries found people searching for a better philosophy. Something was missing in their lives.

Art and Erma wondered if they should take the time to attend the December 1964 missionary conference. However, they were glad they went, because one of the speakers was Dr. Walter Martin, whose lifelong studies of cults was so helpful to the evangelical world. He came to Italy especially to warn the missionaries of the rising danger of false cults. In 1964, the Jehovah's Witnesses had 245 meeting places in Italy, and 6,929 workers (foreign and national).

The Jehovah's Witnesses had gained much ground in Modena, with two meeting places well attended. The Mormons planned to send 100 missionaries to Italy in 1965. New freedom to read the Bible paved the way for these two groups and others to offer their teaching to spiritually dissatisfied people. Both groups called themselves 'evangelical', which confused the average man on the street. The *Voce della Bibbia* staff and local churches ran into this problem frequently. Dr. Martin's messages were helpful, interesting, and challenging as he presented the missionaries with 'know-how' tips on dealing with people caught up in false cults.

Opening one's home to provide housing for traveling preachers is almost a lost art in America. Anyone who grew up sleeping on the floor so traveling evangelists or missionaries could have their bed can tell you about the flip side, the reward of personally getting to know awesome people. The best place to learn about missions is around a dinner table, talking to the missionary face to face while he relates splendid tales. In this casual setting the visitor gives his listeners a chance to probe him with questions large and small.

One of Aunt Betty's pleasant memories is of getting to know and helping to serve many well-known Christian guests, for example, Mr. and Mrs. Theodore Epp of Back to the Bible, Dr. and Mrs. Clarence Jones of HCJB, Angus Hudson, a publisher from London, and many missionaries passing through Europe to or from their fields of service.

A favorite visitor in the Wiens home was Dr. Joseph Springer, Director of the European office of HCJB. He came with his whole family from Geneva, Switzerland to discuss radio and literature ministries. He spoke at Modena and Formigine, and in the evening showed slides from Ecuador, a treat for the Modena young people. Dr. Springer was a singer, his wife an organist. His knowledge of the Spanish language made it easy for him to pronounce Italian, so, coached by Professor Artini for accuracy, during his visits, he went to Florence to record several solos for use on the Italian broadcasts.

A young man named Massimo, a student in Modena, was first contacted at an evangelistic meeting in 1964. He kept coming to meetings, and soon joined the Intervarsity group, but it was not until Easter 1966 that he was saved. Easter Sunday morning Massimo really drank in the message. The following week he came to the *Voce della Bibbia* office to tell the staff that Easter morning during the message he put his trust in Christ.

A few weeks later, Dr. Francis Schaeffer of L'Abri in Switzerland was the speaker at the student meeting in the Wiens home. After a very appropriate study, he led a discussion that lasted until almost midnight. Massimo brought six new students to the Schaeffer meeting, and one, Daniel, continued to attend all the Intervarsity meetings. Massimo asked to be baptized in a river, so this was arranged, and seven carloads of friends drove to a riverside about fifteen miles from Modena. His college friends were there for the baptism and riverside picnic: Daniel, Anselmo, Luciano, Albert, and Carla. In the afternoon, the group went to the

130

meeting at Sassuolo, where Abe Unrau was speaking. To culminate a special day in Massimo's life, the whole gang ended up at the Wiens home, where the fellowship went on all evening.

His first year in Italy Arthur became acquainted with Ernest Migliazza, an Italian missionary who went to an unreached tribe in Brazil. The Modena Assembly had sent offerings for his work several times, so he came to give them a firsthand report. He spoke, showed slides and told about his experiences during ten years in Brazil. Ernest learned the unwritten language of the tribe and translated the book of Mark for them. Massimo planned to become a doctor, and had a burden to become a missionary. The report from Brazil touched him deeply, and increased his resolve to go.

All of the local young people helped out at the *Voce della Bibbia* office on occasion, preparing mailings or tracts for distribution, or other big jobs best done with many hands. The office staff enlarged, so that in addition to Remo Dosi and Nerina Ferrari, Lidia Comune and Valeria Brentan were full-time workers. Betty Jabs, Franca Ferrari, and Lilian Johnson were regular assistants.

The two short-wave broadcasts over Trans World Radio were very effective, even though they were only 15 minutes each, once a week. A 15-minute medium wave broadcast at 11:30 p.m. was exciting, because even though it was late at night, the reception was much better than short wave. In two and a half years, this broadcast brought good responses. Back to the Bible aired their half-hour English program on the same medium wave station at 10:30 p.m. Saturday nights, and in 1966 they gave up this half hour so Italian broadcasting could be expanded. This represented the best radio opportunity yet.

Arthur's follow-up visits took him to new areas in Italy,

131

and he was thrilled with the good responses he was receiving. The Lord was at work through the radio broadcasts! One radio contact he visited in the province of Brescia. The individual sent for the correspondence courses and had completed three of them. He told Arthur that after he had listened to the broadcasts regularly for about a year and had studied the Bible through the courses sent to him he understood the gospel well. During the Christmas broadcast he knelt down, confessed his sins, and asked Christ to save him. He was thrilled to have Art's visit, and had many questions.

As it turned out, this man was an ex-priest. Arthur put him in touch with a Swiss missionary, and he began to faithfully attend all the services and took an active part in the church.

The radio ministry increased the need for more literature. One of the booklets printed for distribution to radio contacts was 'After Death', written by Richard Wolff. A lady in the town of Vicenza heard the radio offer of this booklet at the time her mother was dying of cancer. She immediately wrote to request it. In the next letter she said that she read the booklet to her dying mother, who had never been sure of eternal life. The booklet brought her to the assurance of her salvation.

And in Rome, a very strange story. One evening a Hindu and his Italian wife were watching television when the set gave out. They turned on the radio, where the first words they heard were 'Jesus Christ'. This caught their attention so they continued to listen. It was the Back to the Bible Broadcast in English aired throughout Europe. They wrote in and followed the English correspondence courses they were sent. Since they lived in Italy, their name was sent to *Voce della Bibbia* for follow-up. Arthur had the joy of kneeling down with this elderly Hindu as he prayed and received Christ as his own personal Savior.

Our awesome God! So interested in one individual that He broadcast His Word in English throughout Europe, stopped a television set in Rome so a Hindu from India would turn on his radio, kept his attention through inspiring programs, and when the old man knelt to pray, welcomed him as His child!

Such stories delighted the *Voce della Bibbia* staff as they gathered for their meetings to hear reports, pray, and discuss plans. It is not hard to see why they were such dedicated workers!

Shirley passed her eighth grade. In the Italian school system, this brought her to a time of decision. She could, of course, leave home to complete her studies in America, but she chose to stay in Italy. Beginning with the ninth grade, Italian students choose a school, which determines the courses of study they will follow for the next five years. To be with her friends, Shirley chose Classical High School, the most difficult one. She studied ancient Greek which gave her the ability to read the New Testament in Greek and grade papers for the Greek classes at Columbia Bible College. In her third year she began prayer meetings with her Catholic school mates thus reading the Psalms together.

Shirley accepted the Lord as her Savior at age four, at her grandparents' home in California. When Gloria was five, she met her parents after their day of work at the office to announce that she had asked Jesus to come into her heart. Gloria started first grade in the Italian elementary school where Shirley had gone.

Chapter 8

'The Most Beautiful Story, the Bible'

Shortly after she came to Italy, Erma discovered a truth that shocked her: Italy had no Bible Story Book – not even a little one. It became the prayer of her heart that some day, some way, Italian children would be able to snuggle up to their mom or dad and listen to a bedtime story from God's Word. She prayed that Italian families would have a Bible Story Book to read around the table for daily devotions.

Family devotions were not common in Italy. It soon became evident to the growing community of evangelical missionaries that the greatest need in Italy was for Christian families. There were some Christian homes in Italy. Through the moving of the Holy Spirit, whole families had been saved. Art and Erma discovered such groups in the Sassuolo district, for example, where the fathers were strong spiritual leaders in their homes. Some of the children and young people in the 1950s camps at Poggio Ubertini were from Christian homes. As a rule, however, many new adult converts stood alone in their family, often being the only Christian in the neighborhood, or the whole town.

Betty Jabs recalls the first Sunday she was in Italy. The family was visiting around the dinner table when suddenly Arthur said, 'Quiet now! Aunt Erma will be on in a minute.' Sure enough, a very familiar voice came over the airwaves with warm enthusiasm, *'Ciao Ragazzi! Questa e 'Zia Erma!'*

Although she couldn't understand it, she was touched by the appealing tone of the speaker's voice, the warmth that radiated out to her listeners. Betty thought, 'Surely any child that hears this broadcast will stop to listen!'

Many did listen, and many wrote in. One of the prayers for the broadcast was that adults in the homes would allow children to continue listening. The staff at the *Voce della Bibbia* office realized that most children reached through radio had no Christian support system. The new challenge was to keep children in distant areas interested, children whose only contact was listening to '*Zia Erma*'. The children wrote precious letters telling how much they liked the Sunday afternoon programs. One child wrote that she and her mother set the alarm to remind them of the hour of the broadcast so they wouldn't ever miss it!

From the days of the apostles, letters and home visits have been successful forms of communication. Following World War II, new avenues for spreading the gospel turned up so fast one could scarcely keep current. Evangelicals were not alone in proclaiming a message. So many new ideas were bombarding the minds that anyone wanting to hold the attention of new contacts had to jump on board to keep their message before their intended audience. Nor was using modern methods enough. The speakers were only channels through whom the Holy Spirit worked, and since the work was the Lord's, everyone understood the importance of keeping all aspects of the broadcasts bathed in prayer.

For the first ten or twelve years, the ministry in Modena had been a trudge up a very steep hill. Considering the effort it took to get them, results sometimes seemed relatively small. But as a hiker climbs a mountain one step at a time keeping his eye on the goal, so with the Modena team. As they looked back, they saw the amazing distance they had covered by the grace of God. Not only had many people opened their hearts and homes to the evangelicals, many active church groups had sprung up in surrounding towns. The team was growing, as Italian Christians learned the Word of God, discovered and used their spiritual gifts, and took on the responsibility of helping to win others.

The Modena team rose to the challenge to find ways to draw distant contacts into their embrace. To begin with, outreach was through literature. Everyone who wrote in response to tracts and coupons received a Gospel of John and a correspondence course lesson. This put them into a track that led to writing and receiving letters. Both adults and children wrote frequently, sometimes to say they enjoyed the material, other times to ask questions. And invariably, when the light of understanding dawned and they received Christ as Savior, the *Voce della Bibbia* office would hear about it. Those letters sparked a celebration during staff prayer time. Conversions also led to a need for deeper counseling by letter. The address file was beginning to bulge. The people who responded favorably to the phone book mailing in Modena were also put on the mailing list.

It didn't take long after starting the broadcasts for the mailing department to build up a sizeable list. As time went on, it was clear that some form of automated address list ought to be started. Answer to the prayer for such equipment came in the form of Addressograph and Graphotype machines donated by Back to the Bible Broadcast. They arrived safely in Italy, only to be impounded at the customs office for two months. A Christian at the American Consulate wrote to the director of customs to urge him to release the equipment, and it finally was set up in the office and put to good use. Fifteen-thousand names and addresses were ready to be put onto the metal plates used by this equipment, and more were added every month.

The coupon ministry continued to expand, bringing in hundreds of new contacts and alerting them to the broadcasts. Remo introduced a generic coupon printed by the Conservative Baptist Bookstore in Naples, on which the supplier printed a code. The returned coupons received at Naples could be sent to the distributor. Art's number was 29. The new coupon also offered the free Gospel of John and four-lesson course on John from the Navigators. As before, it concluded with sending a New Testament as reward for completing the lessons, and other courses were offered. The Naples bookstore then asked if they could code all coupons distributed in northern Italy to return to the *Voce della Bibbia* office, which in turn could be picked up by other distributers in the north.

Thus the adult correspondence courses grew, but there was no such course for children writing to 'Aunt Erma'. She had not overlooked this need. In the office she directed workers to note children under sixteen, and keep a separate file for them. When she heard of a four-lesson children's course on John that was successfully used in France, she immediately began the process of preparing the course for use in Italy.

Erma first offered the children's Bible correspondence course in Italian on her broadcasts in Spring, 1962. Eighty-three children enrolled in the first six weeks, and the drop-out rate was much less than in the adult course. This was partly because Aunt Erma sent along a chapter of a story 'to be continued'. Kids wanted the next installment, so a high percentage finished the course.

In 1963 the team decided to begin a bi-monthly magazine. At first a four page bulletin, it was called *Qui' Voce della Bibbia* ("Here is Voice of the Bible"). The bulletin focused on the radio broadcasts announcing future programs and encouraging the reader to listen. It was an inspirational magazine, designed to help them grow in understanding. It also familiarized isolated folks with the radio speakers and their friends at the *Voce della Bibbia* staff. The goal was to draw them into the broader circle of believers, to give them a sense of belonging to the family of God.

One could scarcely imagine who might be listening to the broadcasts. People from every level of society were among them. Gian Nunzio Artini was well loved among the common people, known to many of the listeners from his years as a traveling evangelist. He was often called Professor Artini, because he was a noted music professor. His sweet spirit and gentle mannerisms delighted all who met him, especially the ladies, whom he greeted by bowing to kiss their hand. In every way he showed great respect. This came through in his radio messages, which appealed to the educated, as well as the masses.

Because of the high standards of general literature in Italy, the magazine needed to be top quality. Samuele Negri agreed to be the editor. He assigned articles to various Christians, and wrote many himself, usually without a byline.

In 1964, Erma decided to prepare a calendar to offer on the children's broadcast at the end of the year. The response was wonderful. Letters came from all over Italy and from several other countries where the broadcast was heard.

Giorgio Ferrari married a young woman who became a close friend of Erma's and a volunteer worker in the *Voce della Bibbia* office. Erma and Franca met in 1953 at the Poggio Ubertini Bible camp. She was from a Brethren home in Bologna, but when she and Giorgio began dating, she often came to Modena and attended the Evening Bible School. Along with the other youth, she helped the Wiens in their evangelistic efforts. She taught Sunday school at her church in Bologna, so Erma gave her tips on how to brighten up her classes. She encouraged Franca and all the youth to find their gifts and use them.

After her marriage to Giorgio, Franca became the organist in the Modena church and began helping in the *Voce della Bibbia* office. Erma encouraged her to learn to make wedding cakes for people of the church. This ministry of love started with a Japanese couple who came to Modena, and the contact came through Art's sister Ruth, a missionary in Japan. The couple didn't want a Shinto wedding, so Ruth called Art to see if he would perform the wedding. The church welcomed the couple and many even brought gifts to the wedding. From then on, Franca made the wedding cakes!

Franca was such a radiant Christian. A doctor's wife named Rossana living in the same apartment building watched her go to work each day. She wondered how this young woman could be so happy at eight o'clock in the morning, regardless of the weather – cold, foggy, raining, snowing.

'Where do you work?' she asked Franca one day. 'You always seem so happy to go every morning!'

'I work at *Voce della Bibbia*,' replied Franca. Rossana wanted to know more about this job that made her so happy, so Franca told her about the purpose of the ministry. When they parted, the woman begged her to come back to tell her more.

Franca was not sure of her ability to clearly witness to this woman, so when she went back, she took Erma along. The woman's questions were so deep that Erma suggested to Franca that next time she went, she should take Remo Dosi with her. Remo specialized in explaining the gospel to people who were seeking the truth, and before very many weeks went by, Franca's neighbor accepted Christ as her Savior.

Through this contact, Rossana Marinelli, a talented editor, came to help Erma in preparing a children's magazine, launched in 1966. Called *Il Traguardo* (The Goal), it was a 12-page monthly publication patterned after the Back to the Bible's 'Young Ambassador'. *Il Traguardo* contained an editorial by Aunt Erma, a section called 'Your Problems Answered', a main story, a crossword puzzle, jokes, and an installment of the Danny Orlis stories.

At the beginning, the project was funded by gifts received from donors outside of Italy, but as the months rolled by, funding from within Italy grew. The plan was to make 'The Goal' a subscription magazine. The first issue was sent to everyone on the mailing list under sixteen. Some of the addresses were more than four years old, and of the 8315 sent out, 400 were undeliverable. Only one was marked refused by a nun who said the boy had written without permission. Letters of delight poured in from those who received their first issue.

By the end of one year, 10,000 copies went out monthly. In December 1966, 'Zia Erma' suggested to her listeners that they might send a birthday gift to Jesus to help with the cost of the magazine. Those who responded received a new publication, a comic strip African fable by Dr. Paul White, 'Little Leopards become Big Leopards'. The strip effectively illustrated how little sins become big sins, and it was well received by Italian kids. New literature was continually rolling off the presses in Italy, and readers new and old were constantly reaching out to receive it.

Valeria Brenton's story is quite remarkable. In 1958, the Italian magazine *Epoca* carried an article about the widows of the five missionary martyrs in Ecuador. Valeria, 16 years old, had no idea that the missionaries were Protestant. She

140

was so touched that she wrote to the president of Ecuador to see if she could join Mrs. Elliot in helping the Auca Indians. The president forwarded Valeria's letter to Betty Elliot, a schoolmate of Art's from Wheaton days, who immediately sent Valeria's address to Art Wiens. This began a correspondence between Valeria and the Wiens, and in her second letter, she requested a New Testament and a correspondence course.

When Valeria's family learned about her involvement with the evangelicals, they were very unhappy. Through correspondence, Bible study, and a few visits from Art and Erma, she was converted and grew spiritually. At age 18, she was visited by Art and Silvano, who found that despite severe persecution from her family, her faith was strong. In 1962 they invited her to work at *Voce della Bibbia*. Her father refused to let her go, and arranged with her employer to watch her closely. She was forbidden any contact with evangelicals. Until July 1963, when she turned 21, she was under the father's rule.

Valeria wanted to serve the Lord and they knew they could use her talents at *Voce della Bibbia.* At 22 she asked the Wiens what they thought she should do, and they suggested that she attend Emmaus Bible School in Switzerland. Her parents were furious when she told them her plans. They gave her a half hour to get out of the house. She went to her sister's home, and from there, Art and Erma picked her up. Valeria was a very timid person, but warmed to the love of the Wiens family and office staff. As Valeria recalls those days, she says, 'Erma began taking care of me in the 1960s. I was her spiritual child, and I sometimes hurt her. She never showed any sign of impatience, just love. She wanted me as assistant translator of the Danny Orlis books, and this worked into her asking me to be assistant author of the Bible story book.'"

Valeria, strong in the faith after all her hardship, was a sensitive and creative individual. It didn't take long for her to understand Erma's ministries and to ease into a comfortable working relationship. Valeria added her special touch by editing with her superb Italian style, and the two women made a very good team.

Erma was soon using Valeria to edit other material, which she could translate most efficiently on tape. They developed a smooth system that allowed them to translate high quality material very quickly. In addition to the Bible story on the broadcast, Erma always used an illustrative story – one of the favorites was 'Snowflake', read by Shirley. When she decided to use a continued story, she chose Bernard Palmer's Danny Orlis books. Working from the Italian, Erma would do an instant oral translation, much as an interpreter does when translating for a speaker. One installment at a time went on tape; Valeria would put her creative talent to work and write it with her Italian flair; Erma would read it into the program. Several of the books were thus translated, and later published in Italian.

The next project was a much bigger one. The Bible story book Erma had dreamed of was coming into focus. On two occasions Erma had located talented Italian Christians to write a Bible story book. In the first instance, the project didn't get off the ground. In the second, the individual got as far as Abraham before ill health kept her from going on.

Erma could have found a quiet corner and just written the Bible story book herself, but a book written by a foreigner would have been second best. She believed firmly that no matter how well a foreigner spoke the language, it was always advisable to use Italians for writing. The idioms and nuances of the language are illusive. As her Italian friends often reminded her, speaking and writing in a foreign tongue

142

are two different things. Now at last she had the answer! She would tell the stories on tape, and Valeria could write them. Valeria put her plans for Bible school on hold to work on this exciting project.

Neither of the women recognized what an immense task they had undertaken. At first Erma considered translating an existing story book, such as the Moody Bible Story Book. She decided against that, for although it would have been easier, a book translated into Italian directly from the Bible would be more 'Italian'.

The hubbub of the crowded office with all its interruptions was not the atmosphere for such an important project. Not having the luxury of six months in a mountain hideaway, the girls decided to work in the apartment Valeria shared with Betty Jabs. Betty assured them that as long as they left her bed open for the night, the rest of the apartment was theirs. They spread out their books, typewriters and papers, and went to work. Starting at the beginning, they would read versions of the Bible in Italian, in French, and in English. They would discuss the biblical account at length, and would pray for God to guide their thoughts to create the best possible account of the story at hand.

When they felt they had the story well in their minds, Erma, an accomplished storyteller, would recount it in her own words translating orally with only the accuracy of the story in mind. Valeria would listen one paragraph at a time, and write the material in good Italian style and form. Thus they worked on and on, until they had completed 269 stories. They named the Italian Bible story book: 'The Most Beautiful Story, The Bible'!

With the financial help of Moody Literature Mission and many gifts from donors who had followed the project from its earliest inception, the beautiful Bible story book was published in 1969. Erma's dream became a reality, as thousands of copies went out into Italian homes. *La Storia Piu Bella, La Bibbia* was promoted widely through radio and literature, and was carried in many bookstores.

In September 1968, Arthur traveled to Ireland where he was invited to speak at the Belfast Worldwide Missionary Conference, the Vittoria Brethren Assembly Missionary Conference, a meeting of the Gideons, and several other meetings. During the ten days he was gone, Erma, Aunt Betty, and Art's sister Ruth from Japan took Gloria and Shirley, with five of Shirley's friends, to camp at Zermatt, Switzerland. Through the kindness of Swiss friends they had the use of a chalet on the side of the mountain in full view of the majestic Matterhorn.

This was an exciting adventure for the girls, and the weather cooperated, making it possible to see all the beautiful scenery and enjoy the mountain hikes. Even though the girls came from different backgrounds, they got along harmoniously. Shirley's best friend Maria, for whom she had so often prayed, was along. There also was the social butterfly, Paola who was from a very wealthy home. All of them were lovely, sweet girls.

As a missionary, Ruth worked with Japanese students for eighteen years. With Erma translating, she led the girls in Bible reading and had many significant discussions with them. They were intensely interested in life in Japan. After hearing Erma's testimony, Paola said, 'But it's really difficult to find God!' Four of the girls, including Maria and Paola, agreed to start a high school Bible study in the Wiens home in the fall.

Erma was relaxed for the ten days, which in her mind meant making the knitting needles fly. In the car, on the mountain trails, walking down into town to buy groceries, 'the knitting lady' never dropped a stitch. In fact, wasting time was not allowed in Erma's life. Back in Modena she always asked Aunt Betty to accompany her when she went downtown, to watch the car while she ran in. Before they left home she would ask the Lord to save a parking space for them, because they couldn't afford to waste time circling around looking for a space. 'And,' laughs Betty, 'we almost always found a spot right away!'

As a result of the growing radio ministry and related projects, by 1968, over 40,000 adults had requested Gospels of John and four thousand had completed the correspondence course lesson, receiving a New Testament as their reward. Many went on to more advanced lessons. The *Voce della Bibbia* office needed additional space, and additional staff. The latter came in the form of two missionary women from Naples, Teddy and Skippy (Misses Scipione and Tedesco), who sang at the Wiens' wedding fifteen years earlier. They settled in the town of Reggio Emilia where doors were opening, and helped in Modena speaking at the ladies' meetings, holding children's rallies, and in office work. Skippy took over the accounts of *Voce della Bibbia*, freeing Arthur for more ministry of visitation.

As to office space, the end of February 1969 they moved into a spacious office. Gloria was ecstatic when she heard that the carpenter coming to remodel the building to suit their needs was none other than Grandpa Plato from Calgary, Alberta. The Platos were scheduled to remain through June. In this, the fifth year at the Modena fair, most of the staff joined Ewalt Plato, hammering, painting, varnishing to give the booth at the fair a new look. Thousands of pieces of literature were given out, but the most effective witness was the personal conversations various ones had with people who stopped to talk. Many had purchased Bibles in previous

145

years; some received the magazines and many told of listening to various broadcasts.

As the 1960s gave way to the 1970s the whirlwind of activities continued, and increased. Personal notes include the weddings of two staff members. Ellero married Lidia, and they settled in Modena. Massimo married Tina, who had replaced Valeria as translation assistant, and moved to Bologna. The gifts needed for this ministry were unique, and brought Erma to her knees asking the Lord for a new helper.

Gloria surprised Aunt Betty one day by telling her how very much she wanted a baby brother. 'But Aunt Betty,' she said, 'I just can't pray for one because Mama is so busy. It is not possible. If she had a baby to care for who would do the radio broadcasts and write for *Il Traguardo*?'

Aunt Betty reminded her that when she was very small, Aunt Betty came to take care of her and to help Mama.

'Well then,' reasoned Gloria, 'I could pray for a baby after all!'

What Gloria didn't know was that before she called, God had answered. Erma's baby was expected in November, and while she was very, very pregnant, the family took a group of young people on a once-in-a-lifetime summer Bible camp to Spain, even crossing over into Morocco.

Daniel Wiens was born November 18, 1970. Grandpa Plato decided his carpentry skills were needed in Italy again, and Grandma was sure she could find something to do. After Grandma Plato left, Gloria saw that Aunt Betty was indeed capable of caring for Daniel. After two months, Erma entrusted her baby to Aunt Betty and went back to her busy pace. Aunt Betty was delighted. The best part of her job had just begun.

Arthur's report for *Voce della Bibbia* after nine years showed that 132,205 pieces of mail had been received. Radio listeners from all of Italy's 94 provinces had written, as well as people from 20 other countries. Fifty thousand persons had mailed in coupons requesting the correspondence Bible course in John, and 2,845 adults and 3,076 children had completed the course.

The Wiens were so pressed from every side with so much work and the urgent need for staff replacement was weighing heavily on them. A chance to laugh was a gift one day, from an answer written by one of the students doing the correspondence course. The verse to look up was John 3:16, and the question was, 'What was God's gift to man which proved His great love?' One man answered, 'He created woman.'

Chapter 9

'In Prison, and Ye Visited Me'

By the late 1960s, Art Wiens knew a great many city and regional officials in Modena. From his earliest contacts in trying to establish residence there, and over the years, he made friends among the police. Through introductions and by conducting business, he also became acquainted with people in high government offices. His brother Jim Wiens, recalling his visits to Italy says, 'Everybody in Modena knows Art. He took me on a tour, and as we neared a Catholic church an older gentleman – the priest – came running out to greet him. We went to a Catholic bookstore. The owner embraced him. Then he took us to another shop owned by a "hippy". The shop was filled with items that would attract the hippy culture, but the young man had a glowing testimony for the Lord. Another time we stopped at a gas station where the attendant greeted Art like an old buddy.'

Art had indeed made friends all over, close friends, for in addition to being a 'people person', he made friendship evangelism his goal. As with every area of the Wiens' ministry, prisons in other towns were open to Art, but in sixteen years, despite knowing key people, he had never been able to get his foot in the door of the Modena prison.

Way back in 1956, a man named Rocco in southern Italy opened his home for evangelical meetings. Word of this event spread throughout the Christian community. It was considered a big victory, because Rocco was a rough character, not the type to be interested in Bible study. However, four years later he committed a serious crime and was sentenced to twenty-seven years in prison. He was sent north, to the Reggio Emilia prison. A cousin gave him a Bible and Jehovah's Witness books.

In America, this cult preys on disillusioned Protestant church goers; in Italy, they found disillusioned Catholics, people genuinely searching for the truth. Missionaries there found that the Bibles given to individuals by cults were often used to open their eyes to the truth of the gospel. So it was with Rocco. Before he ever met an evangelical, he studied the Bible given to him by his cousin, put his faith in Christ, and came to the conclusion that the Jehovah's Witness teaching was in error.

He wrote to the *Voce della Bibbia* office to order a songbook, saying he had received their address from a tract.. In response, Arthur visited Rocco and continued the contact by correspondence. A British missionary living in Reggio Emilia, Godfrey Miller kept up the personal visits. Evangelicals also started him on Bible correspondence courses and introduced him to the Navigators' Bible memory program. He went on to do eight correspondence courses, and through reading a book on prayer, began to pray regularly from 4:00 a.m. to seven every morning.

Voce della Bibbia had contact with nine prisoners at the time, two others in the same prison as Rocco, and his firm commitment to the Lord was a help to them.

The doors to the Modena prison opened to Art Wiens big time December 5, 1969. The headline on his morning newspaper and the pictures on the front page shocked him. Four young people, three of them Americans, had been arrested in Modena the night before on drug charges. They were imprisoned in Modena awaiting trial.

'You've got to go see them, Art,' exclaimed Erma.

'I have to try,' replied Art. 'But you know how many times they've turned me down!'

'But these are Americans! And look, the girls are so young!'

One of the girls arrested was from New Zealand. Helen, only 22, found herself incarcerated in Modena, locked up in a dingy room with three Italian prisoners, hard-looking women who didn't know her language. The American girl, Carolyn, was in another cell; she had no idea where Doug and Richard were. Whether from ignorance or faith, jailed in a Catholic country Helen began praying that God would send her a Protestant minister. Finally in a magazine she found the address of a minister in London. She wrote to him, but had no money for a stamp.

Unknown to Helen, a minister was on his way, trying to get permission to see the young people imprisoned on drug charges. He was praying for success based on the fact that three of them were Americans, and that God would be pleased for him to witness to them. He was about to enter the toughest ministry of his whole career.

Richard Ford, the leader of the four, could hardly be considered young. He was 42, a fugitive from the law hiding out in Europe and North Africa, wanted on narcotics charges in the U.S. His first marriage, to a German girl, was good, especially after he quit drinking. However, unknown to his wife Elsa, he had simply switched from liquor to marijuana. In 1962, Richard was arrested at the Mexican border for trying to bring marijuana into the United States. He was sentenced to five years in prison. Elsa came to visit him often and brought the baby, and when she couldn't come, she wrote every day. She worked, saving as much as she could, waiting for his release.

He came home after three and a half years. Because of his prison record and his age he believed it would be hard to find a job, so he decided to set up a shop of his own. Taking all of Elsa's hard-earned savings, he set up a shop to cater to the hippies, youth who were trying to express 'an honest love'. He wanted to be part of that scene, because even though marijuana had put him in prison, he believed it was good. It had, after all, stopped his drinking.

One day friends of Richard's came into the shop and asked him to try LSD with them. A different person took over his body and mind. Within three months he realized he was hooked on LSD, craving it and taking it again and again. He became a zombie, walking and talking love. Elsa was beside herself, and finally, in desperation, she divorced him.

Even then, he believed he could return to her once he had fulfilled his mission. He had to figure out who he was and where he was going. But when he tried to reason, something pushed it all out of his mind. He could no longer reason.

Carolyn had been using LSD long before she met Richard. They moved in together and lived on a daily dose of drugs. There was no longer a world around them; they just stayed high. In time, Carolyn became pregnant. A spark of decency left in Richard made him stay by her until their little boy was born. Pity and some shred of honesty kept them together.

Richard was arrested again on marijuana charges. When he was released on bond, he knew that on this second offense he would be sentenced to ten years in prison. He skipped the country, heading for Germany. Carolyn left her baby in Chicago and met him there. Together they traveled to Morocco, where they met Helen and Douglas.

Like a lot of young people in the 1960s, Helen had left home with three companions to travel, seeking adventure. They made their way from New Zealand to Germany, then to

151

London, and finally south across France and Spain, en route to the fascinating country of Morocco. As they neared Morocco they talked about hashish, or 'kif', well known among transient youth seeing the world during the 60s.

Helen wasn't sure about drugs. She had no experience, not even with alcohol, since no one in her family drank. Her female companion had made up her mind. No drugs. She connected them with evil, with the 'white slave' trade rumored to snatch white girls and imprison them in harems. One of the Australian men in the foursome said he thought it would be all right to try hashish, if given the opportunity. His philosophy, as he talked on, made sense to Helen, and she liked his decisiveness.

From Gibraltar they crossed over to Morocco on a ferry, and began making their way across the country, finally arriving in the picturesque city of Marrakech, in southern Morocco. At the entrance to a campground where they planned to set up their tent, they met a man called Momo, finally someone who spoke English! Momo took Helen through the ancient *Kasbah*, the old walled-in section of the city, to a cafe. Seeing that she was interested in the long clay pipe, Momo offered to let her try it. He stuffed it with hashish and lit it, finally handing it to her. She puffed on it timidly and handed it back.

'No, no!' cried Momo, 'you have to take a deep breath and inhale a big puff to get the benefit of this fine hashish! Here, try again!'

Helen took a big puff, and then panic set in. The music of the juke box, the sweet smelling odor of hashish, the raucous laughter of the rough looking crowd in the cafe frightened her. She jumped up and ran all the way back to the safety of the campground, losing a shoe along the way.

Through a series of travels, Helen found herself living

with her companions in a Moroccan home in Oujda, a northern city on the border of Algeria. One day at the post office she saw a curious looking vehicle, a Volkswagen bug with the word 'LOVE' painted across the front of it. The weird individual driving it called to her, 'Do you speak French?'

Helen looked him over. Until this trip she had been rather sheltered so she knew little about the hippy culture. He appeared to be about forty, with long hair and beard, unkempt clothes, and beads. His female companion seemed quite young. 'Maybe I can help you,' she replied. Arabic was the language of Morocco, but some people spoke Spanish and French as well. Communicating in a mixture of languages, she did her best to explain to the postal clerk that this man, Richard Ford, was inquiring about a money order he expected from America. The clerk indicated that nothing had come for a Richard Ford as yet, but perhaps it would arrive soon. Richard seemed pleased.

Helen invited Richard and Carolyn to come and meet the Moroccan man at the home where she was staying. He operated a place known as a 'crash-pad', where transient hippies were welcome to spend the night. 'You can spread your sleeping bags on the floor, as we do,' she told them, 'and stay as long as you'd like.'

The invitation sounded good to the pair. They went with Helen and soon were settled comfortably on cushions on the floor of a beautifully tiled Moroccan sitting room. When the evening meal was over, the sparse furniture was pushed back and candles lit to give the room a subtle atmosphere. The guests were reclining on cushions on the floor when the pipe filled with tobacco and hashish was passed around. Everyone relaxed except Helen. The headiness brought on by the hashish made her nervous, but at the same time, she felt at

153

peace. She recalls, 'The strangeness of the darkened room combined to create the intrigue of an old movie. Should I stay, or should I run, try to get away from it all? Could I make that choice, or were my choices already made?'

She stayed, and soon her focus was on Richard, who began telling fascinating stories. In the candlelight he looked like a prophet, scraggly long hair, deeply lined face, beard, weird outfit, and beads. His voice seemed almost enchanted, compelling her to listen.

Before too many days went by, Richard asked Carolyn for a loan. Believing that his money order was on the way and she would soon get it back, she gave him some money. As the sultry summer days slowly drifted by, the money order didn't come. Naively Helen found herself discussing another loan with Richard, who offered a camera (he never produced) for collateral. She gave him the remainder of her traveler's checks. She fully expected to be reimbursed when his money came from the United States.

No money came. Instead, another pair of Americans showed up. They drove a Corvette, and they said they were from Chicago. Like Richard, their motives for coming to Morocco were other than tourism. The lovely landscapes, captivating dark eyes of the Moroccan women, and interesting sights were far from their minds. Some kind of a deal was made, sealed with a handshake, and the boys from Chicago settled in. Hush-hush conversations resulted in secretive activity, but although Helen noticed it, it didn't seem to concern her.

Another American found the crash-pad, and Douglas soon picked up on cultural clues that pointed to questionable business deals. Douglas was beginning to care about Helen, and he had reason to believe that the company they were in was up to no good.

'Come on, Helen,' he coaxed, 'this place isn't safe for you! Please, come with me. We'll leave and go to Spain!'

'They owe me a lot of money,' she argued. 'No way will I leave until I get my money!'

'You must leave,' he insisted. 'This is dangerous company!' But it was to no avail.

If only Helen had listened to Douglas! Whatever he suspected, he was right that Richard Ford was not good company. One day Richard made a deal with Helen. The Chicago boys, along with Richard and Carolyn, were going back to Germany by way of Algeria, across Tunisia, where they would take a ferry over to Sicily. In exchange for her loans to him, she could travel with them.

Helen would have preferred getting her money back, but she was not about to let them get away without paying her. She decided to go along. Since Douglas couldn't sway her, he joined the caravan, too, to protect her.

The trip across North Africa was intense – four people crowded into the Volkswagen bug chugging up and down Morocco's mountainous west, speeding across the farmlands, sweating through the desert to Algeria. The Corvette brought up the rear. It was beastly hot and dusty, but as they neared the first border, they freshened up and combed their hair, the men tucking their long locks under their hats.

The Americans got visas at the border easily because of the favored status of their country. Helen, being from New Zealand, had trouble. It took a bribe plus considerable fast talking to get her through.

Northern Algeria sped by, the mud houses of villages almost blending in to the countryside. Late that night they reached Algiers, a big enough city to find lodging, food, and a to protect the cars from vandalism. They traveled on to Tunisia, and as planned, after a ferry trip across to Palermo,

Sicily, the two men from Chicago went on their way.

Richard, Carolyn, Douglas and Helen – Helen later referred to them as 'the Modena Four', were alone. Palermo seemed interesting so they did some sight-seeing. Somehow Richard sneaked a human skull from the catacombs, and later that night, without explaining to his companions why, sneaked it back in. They moved on across Italy to Rome, stopping again for sight-seeing, and then headed north. Their destination was Modena.

With no religious upbringing to guide her, and no familiar authority to stop her, Helen relaxed and slipped easily into each evening's round of hashish. When LSD was brought out, she and Douglas tried that too, and enjoyed hours of rhapsody with no sleep that night. They were still on a happy high all the next day, window shopping at the beautiful department stores of Florence. By the time they reached Modena, they were both enjoying daily drugs.

Richard's Volkswagen broke down in Modena, and because their money was running out, they settled in a *pensione* (an old-fashioned inn). 'We're all part of the same family,' said Richard that night, 'and we should all help to provide for our needs.' This was his way of saying it was time for Douglas and Helen to peddle the product. They found a cafe teaming with university students, and began to make conversation. One young man, obviously from a wealthy family, became very friendly. He invited them to his home, a very elegant home. Helen observed that there was nothing sordid about peddling marijuana, nothing that seemed illegal. It was just a friendly act of sharing a good thing.

The Italian told them that since he was son of an influential man, he wanted no one to find out about his purchase. They agreed not to tell and in turn he promised to find them other buyers whom he would refer to the *pensione* where they were staying.

They had made a sale! They went home happy. If they could just find a few more 'brothers' to buy from them, they could soon be on the road again.

That night, December 4, 1969, as the four relaxed in their room, there was a 'knock, knock' on their door. It was the police.

Art and Erma determined to contact these American young people. Even though he knew he was beating against a cement wall, Art decided he would do all he could to get into the prison. He made his way to the prison director's office, and was turned down. The director did suggest that he might try a higher official. Again he was turned down, with the suggestion that he appeal to yet another official. It took him from 9:00 a.m. until 1:00 p.m., but on December 6, he walked through the prison gates and awaited his turn with the crowd of folks gathered to visit relatives and friends.

That first day, Arthur was allowed to see only Richard and Douglas. He was allotted 30 minutes, and he sat quietly and listened to them rage at him, making rude, angry comments, as they mocked his beliefs. Richard recalled, 'Right away I saw through this guy. Keeping my little flock together I told them, "We are far above this man." I would talk to him about Aquarius, and believe me, I used all the power in my mind to try and weaken him and drive him away.... The force in me was after him in every way, to hurt and shame and break him.'

When Art's half hour was running out, he quietly told the two men about the love of Jesus, and offered to give them tracts and to bring them New Testaments. They tore up the tracts and walked away.

From then on, almost every Saturday morning Art went to the tribunal for permission, and then to the prison, where he had to wait his turn to get in. He sometimes took others with him, always praying for a break in their stubborn attitudes. For the first five months he only saw Richard and Douglas, some weeks together, other weeks one or the other. He obtained permission for a woman working with Intervarsity to visit the girls. Richard and Carolyn told the prison authorities that they were married, so they were given a half-hour together each week. Encouraged by this, Douglas and Helen said they were engaged. This got them the coveted half hour, where they compared notes on the minister's visits.

Through the Intervarsity woman visiting the girls, Art learned that Helen seemed to be searching for the truth. At last he was able to make arrangements to see them. At last, April 27, Helen and Carolyn were brought in to see the minister Helen had waited so long to meet. The following month, he saw Helen alone. She was receptive to the message of the gospel and treasured the literature he left. Before he saw her again, she wrote him a long letter saying she had accepted the Lord as her Savior.

The trial was coming up in August, and Richard was sure that Helen's 'conversion' was just a ploy to get help from Mr. Wiens for early release.

Skippy and Teddy, missionary women at Reggio Emilia, were following Art's prison visits closely. At the trial, Art, Teddy, Skippy, and Shirley sat with the American Counsel from Florence. To Richard's surprise, they did nothing at all to help Helen. But she was set free.

It took a lot of convincing to get Helen to come to the Wiens home when she was released, but Erma was waiting to give her a mother's welcome. Helen had a good soaking bath and shampoo, a wonderful meal, a clean bed to sleep in, and fresh clothes for her trip the next day to the New Zealand Embassy in Rome.

As Thanksgiving neared, Richard told Douglas, 'I sure wish I had a piece of pumpkin pie!'

'This is Italy!' chided Douglas. 'They don't know what pumpkin pie is! But go ahead and pray for it. It's so impossible that if we get pumpkin pie, we'll know there is a God.'

Although Thanksgiving was not an Italian holiday, Erma invited Skippy and Teddy to come for dinner. Skippy said to Teddy, 'Wouldn't it be nice to make a pumpkin pie for the Americans in prison for Thanksgiving?'

When they arrived at the Wiens home Thanksgiving morning, she had a pumpkin pie in her hand. After dinner Art took her through the process of getting permission to deliver the pie. Normally the officials would examine food items brought in, but after an elaborate explanation of the American holiday tradition, the pumpkin pie was taken directly to the American prisoners. There was a God! It was the first chink in the hard armor of the two men!

Carolyn, Douglas and Richard also eventually received Christ. Richard took much longer than the rest. When the others were converted he felt abandoned, and wondered first what was wrong with them, and finally what was wrong with himself. He came to the Lord on Arthur's forty-third visit, a year after he was arrested! He was given a two and a half year sentence in Italy. Helen, Carolyn and Douglas went one by one to L'Abri in Switzerland, where Francis and Edith Schaeffer could minister to them and help them get established in the faith, and on the road to useful lives. Douglas was a graphic artist, and he returned to help with publications at *Voce della Bibbia*, traveling from Switzerland when needed. The Italian government would not grant him permission to stay. Douglas returned to the United States and married a Christian girl. Carolyn's faith was unsteady. She returned to the U.S. as well, and married there, but wavered in her faith.

Upon his release, Richard was returned to California to serve his prison sentence there. He gave a clear testimony that helped many understand the dangers of drugs. The LSD had damaged his mind and he did not completely recover from the effects of his long years of using it.

Helen married, and is now Helen Clare Smith, with an outstanding lifetime career as a missionary in Costa Rica. She and Art Wiens still keep in touch by letter. They have lost track of the other three members of the group, but they pray for them, and keep hoping that they may someday locate them.

Even Art's daughter was impressed with his perseverance in visiting the prisoners. She commented to her father, 'Now, Dad, you are really doing missionary work!' He admits that it was the hardest assignment the Lord ever gave him, but he looks back on it with joy and satisfaction, knowing it was all worthwhile.

The Lord had one more prisoner for Art to contact. An Italian girl arrested in the United States in 1969 became a highly guarded federal prisoner. Silvia Baraldini, from the Modena province, was convicted of terrorism and sentenced to 43 years, sent first to the penitentiary at Lexington, Kentucky. Art began corresponding with her, and over the years sent birthday cards and other greetings. She has responded occasionally. When she underwent cancer surgery, Art sent her a get well card and told her about Erma's cancer. Silvia sent Erma a card.

For many years the Italian government tried to get Silvia transferred to an Italian prison. At last in 1999, the U.S. agreed to move Silvia Baraldini from Danford, Connecticut to Rome, with a promise from Italy that she would be kept in a high security prison for the remaining eight years of her sentence.

Because of his advancing age, Art rarely went to Rome, so he asked a church leader there to go see her, and to give her his greetings. The man exclaimed, 'You don't know Rome! Everything is hard here!'

Art replied, 'I know. All of Italy is hard.'

Hard, yes. But with God, not impossible!

Chapter 10

Life on the Fast Track

The 1970s were busy, wonderful years for evangelicals in Italy. As there were increased numbers of enthusiastic young missionaries, so there was a growing community of gifted young Italians eager to serve the Lord. A network of Italian believers developed between youth who attended Bible camps and conventions together as adolescents and teens. Keeping in touch and seeing one another year after year, they encouraged each other, strengthening the total body of believers. This became a pool of dedicated workers to staff various Christian enterprises throughout Italy. It also spawned Christian homes, as romances developed between believers.

Good things were happening as well among young people who had not been reached during their childhood or teens. In October 1975, five young adults were baptized in Modena. Only one of them, Giancarlo, had been to camp. While he was in high school with Shirley, he was deeply involved in politics, but later turned to Christ. His testimony was strong, and he was burdened for the work among students and other young people. He met his American girlfriend, Helen, when she came to Italy with Shirley one summer to help in the work. Giancarlo married Helen. He became a doctor and practices in Modena.

Marco was contacted through a tent meeting, and then

attended a Bible study and prayer meeting regularly. He shared what he got at the meetings with his friends, so his girlfriend, Laura, and his friend Fabio both became interested. All three of them were saved and they were baptized together. Any church anywhere would have been delighted to have Marco, Fabio and Giancarlo, three enthusiastic Christians, to work with youth! This 'dream team' lifted the Wiens' load in many ways.

Laura became a pharmacist and worked in her mother's shop, while Marco, who became a well loved radio speaker, worked at *Voce della Bibbia*. Fabio became a professor of gymnastics, and eventually a strong leader in the Modena church.

The fifth person baptized that day was Rossana Marinelli, the woman won to Christ through Franca Ferrari's radiant testimony. As it turned out, Rossana was a gifted writer and artist whose contribution to the youth magazine *Il Traguardo* was outstanding. By the mid-1970s it was a 16-page two-color magazine, sent to 14,000 readers. Rossana wrote delightful stories and occasional articles that had the authentic Italian flavor. Her hand in planning the covers and the artistic part of the layout gave it extra appeal. She was an idea person, with unique, original plans month after month. Some of her stories were eventually published in a book, so she became one of Italy's first Christian authors.

Rossana's husband was invited to accompany her to Sweden for a translation convention, and while there, through the witness of a Danish brother, he was converted. Dr. Marinelli came back to Modena transformed. He joined his wife and two little sons in church, a beautiful picture of what prayer can do.

After ten years of traveling to Florence each month for recording programs, in 1972 a studio was set up in Modena.

163

Duke (Stuart) Shelley came from Marseille to Modena once a month to work as part time technician to set up the studio. Duke was a missionary on loan to Back to the Bible Broadcast from Global Outreach. He often quipped that he hoped that the guy coming to work as technician would approve of what he was doing. Then, to Art and Erma's surprise, they received a call from Marseille in December 1972. Duke and Joyce Shelley had been praying about moving to Modena, so he could take over the job as full time technician. Things were worked out, and in January 1973, they settled with their three boys in an apartment in Modena. Joyce, a pianist and typist, found a niche in the ministry as well.

About the time the Shelleys were ready to leave for furlough, GMU missionaries Dave and Judy Hansen came to Modena. While studying language, Dave also took up the work as technician. Dave was on hand to make the move of the studio to a location across town.

One of the most exciting events of this decade was the explosion of small local FM radio stations. These were started by people using surplus equipment left after World War II, cheap, and widely available, and they were a direct challenge to the government monopoly on radio and television. The first stations were started to broadcast rock and roll music. No sooner would the police close a station and confiscate the equipment, than they would be back on the air, the transmitters installed in farm homes, in a hay mow, or in some old building. The first FM station on the air was in Parma, and not long after, one was started in Modena. Several dozen stations went on the air in 1975.

With the help of local believers, *Voce della Bibbia* started broadcasting on these secular, 24 hour radio stations. By the end of 1976 there were 100 FM stations on the air located

164

throughout Italy, including the first Christian station in the province of Varese, in northern Italy. By the end of 1977, 500 FM stations were on the air. By the end of 1982 there were 3,000, some of them quite powerful, owned by large commercial interests. To start a station, one only had to register with the police and be given an unused frequency.

Before long, churches began asking if they could put up Christian radio stations. The technicians of *Voce della Bibbia* scouted out equipment and helped interested church groups find an empty frequency and a suitable location for their transmitter and antenna. Often in one day a station could be set up. In the spring of 1977, they helped put up stations in Trieste, Milan, Florence, and Pisa. In late 1977, *Radio Risposta* (Radio the Answer) was opened by the Modena church. Of the 3,000 stations, sixty of them were Evangelical, most of them on 24-hours a day to keep others from horning in on their frequency.

In January 1976, a call came from Rome advising the Wiens that the evangelicals had decided to start programs each day on a station in Rome. They asked how many spots *Voce della Bibbia* would like to fill. They immediately took two spots, and soon they started receiving mail from Rome. These results encouraged them to contact other secular stations. The Monte Carlo shortwave station was secular. Trans World Radio purchased blocks of time on which they aired Christian programs. The Italians who listened to rock music transmitted by Monte Carlo were familiar with *Voce della Bibbia* programs. Now operating local FM stations, they needed quality programming to fill their hours. When approached, some of them agreed to carry *Voce della Bibbia* programs.

As the years went by, *Voce della Bibbia* experienced the usual turnover of employees. Some seemed irreplaceable, but each time the Lord sent capable new people to take their places. Opportunities arose for various ones to take part in the radio programs, especially as live programs developed. Remo Dosi and Rossana Marinelli agreed to do programs on two television spots offered to *Voce della Bibbia* – a whole new field, an opportunity too good to lose.

Twenty-four hour a day programming for the new Christian stations was a big challenge. The technicians at *Voce della Bibbia* provided stereo 8-track players and cassettes with programs on them, which Christian stations could repeat during the twenty-four hours. One of the technicians worked with an electronic company in Modena to make a small computer for programming to be used by the stations. This brought about a great improvement and helped to provide more variety.

Music was a weak area until the staff learned where to find it. Many young Italian musicians were ready to perform, and they started to come forward. One group after another came to record several numbers, practiced to perfection for radio broadcasting. The music needed to catch listeners turning the dial, to hold their attention, and to give out the Christian message of the song. That they succeeded in reaching their goal is apparent in this letter:

'I am truly enthusiastic about your programs to which I happened to tune in about three months ago. I find myself meditating attentively on what dear Marco says, with his pleasant Emilian accent, sweet voiced Rossana, gentle Aunt Erma and "convincing" Samuele and Vittoria and the others, too, including the singing songwriters and the other young people whose songs praise our beloved Lord Jesus.'

The Modena Christian station, *Radio Risposta*, could be heard as far as 50 miles away, where a man named Bruno

166

owned a pizza restaurant. He made pizza from 2:00 p.m. to 2:00 a.m., and he was looking for something to listen to on the radio while he worked in the kitchen. He found *Radio Risposta*, and since he had never had contact with believers or with the Bible, he was intrigued. Six days a week he listened during the entire 12-hour period. He wrote to request that someone visit him, and Art Wiens was the one who had the privilege of being the first Christian Bruno ever met. Bruno asked many questions during the four hours they were together. He told Art that he had already put his trust in Christ, as the gospel had been explained on the radio. He longed to see an evangelical church established in his town of 15,000.

An 18-year old girl wrote, 'One evening I was turning the knob of the radio, looking for I don't know what, when I discovered your program. I listened carefully....'

Another wrote, 'I would like to offer you my sincere thanks for the spiritual help you give me through the correspondence courses and printed matter that you send me, and above all, for the radio broadcasts. *Voce della Bibbia* is especially close to my heart because, thanks to it, I began to really know the Lord Jesus, and now I have received Him into my heart.'

As radio broadcasts multiplied, the *Voce della Bibbia* office was inundated with letters, excellent feedback from listeners who were hungry for the truth. Correspondence, including the adult and youth magazines, helped maintain contact with scattered radio listeners. People living in cities where strong Christian centers existed were directed to various evangelical groups who could draw new believers into their fellowship.

This still left hundreds of listeners in unreached areas of Italy and in neighboring countries without personal contact.

The need for a roving pastor/counselor was apparent from the start. God had His man ready. Arthur Wiens, experienced, competent and persevering, found immense satisfaction in visiting new homes. With joy he added hours to his day, increased days away from his family, and clocked many miles on his car to visit radio listeners.

Almost always, his trips combined visits to a given region with travels for other purposes. En route to see a printer in Naples he made stops in Rome and other places. If his travels took him to Europe for a camp or convention, he took along his list of radio contacts. If speaking engagements at churches or conventions were scheduled, he called on listeners along the way. Sometimes the need to visit listeners determined his speaking schedule, so he wrote churches asking them to set up meetings for him. He knew and visited with many different churches, whatever Protestant church was within reach of his ministry. He made a point to reach as many Brethren churches as possible.

Art and Erma didn't choose to align themselves with the Brethren. The Brethren, very active in France, Switzerland, and Italy from the earliest years, enveloped them. Their first ministry during language school centered around Intervarsity, which met at the Brethren orphanage for Bible studies, and early Sunday mornings at the Brethren church for prayer. Maria Teresa, who was Brethren, invited Erma to join her in the Brethren camp ministry, which put the Wiens in touch with Brethren people all over Italy. The administrative director of the Brethren Churches in Italy had twice helped them obtain visas.

The only evangelicals in the province of Modena when they arrived were the groups begun by Ettore Barozzini. Since he was Brethren, the meetings he began followed the Brethren form of worship, which lent itself beautifully to house churches where there was no trained leader. Their purpose in discipling new converts was to guide them into Bible study, prayer, and witnessing. Mature Christian men of each group took turns preaching. Elders were elected to handle church leadership. The influence of Barozzini spread to other churches in neighboring towns.

Remo Dosi, a good speaker and a strong leader, led the Modena congregation into the Brethren Assembly. Art and Erma were comfortable with this church decision.

Godfrey Miller, during fifteen years in Reggio Emilia, started two Brethren Assemblies there. He had Evangelical Finnish Lutheran youth groups come to help, and they invited Mauro Bertani to attend seminary in Finland. When he came home he began a Lutheran church in a home in Reggio Emilia.

Meanwhile, evangelicals elsewhere in Italy were starting other churches. One of Art's best friends, Alfredo Del Rosso, planted Nazarene churches. Maria Teresa DeGuistina married Art's friend from Wheaton, Bill Standridge. Along with an impressive literature ministry, they started a Bible church in Rome. Dick Paul, along with Bob Jones was radio technician in the second studio set up at the Brethren orphanage. He went with Art to visit the home where he had his very first Bible study in the 50s. The wife, Dina, was a believer, but her husband was still a communist. Dick offered to resume Bible studies in their home, which resulted in Enzo's conversion and the planting of a Bible church in that part of Florence.

Aside from the Brethren, the only other evangelical group to establish enduring work in the Modena province was the Assembly of God. Like the Southern Baptists, they are very active throughout southern Italy.

All of the mainline denominations remained active. Some

of them (including the Waldensians) went through a very liberal era. Italians, friendly, passionate people, gravitated toward lively evangelical meetings where they could express themselves and use their talents. Church growth and the planting of new churches occurred mainly through evangelical groups.

As frequently as he could, Arthur made repeat visits to radio listeners to help establish them in the faith. While his ministry to them was that of a pastor/counselor, his ministry to scattered churches was that of a guest Bible teacher. Rural areas of Italy in the 1970s were somewhat isolated. Guest speakers rarely passed through, and the churches had no access to Christian bookstores. Art applied for a colportage license so he could provide this service. Then he loaded his car with all the newest books, Bible commentaries, study helps, children's stories and Bibles, and set up a book table in each church he visited.

He planned to arrive in each place early, nine or ten in the morning. His routine was to visit literature and radio contacts in the town, usually taking someone from the church with him. Each visit might be quite different, depending on the age and situation of those in the family. Art liked to have a Bible study in homes that welcomed him, allowing all who were present an opportunity to ask questions or share their thoughts before he closed in prayer. His main joy was to train those who could continue home Bible studies, and to teach them to witness. The visits were often a training ground for this activity. Not all visits were friendly. He got his share of negative feedback at the door, as well. When he left an area, he gave the names and addresses he had not contacted to one of the churches to carry on the follow-up.

His schedule usually allowed for a meeting every night of the week, since he went out for two-week periods in hopes of visiting as many as possible. The special meeting in the evening generally would be well attended, an event the church was looking forward to. After they sang several missionary songs, Arthur would give a fifteen-minute Bible study, and update the church on current news from *Voce della Bibbia*. He would present the latest books on the literature table. He always thanked people who listened regularly to the broadcasts and reminded them to invite their friends to listen. He encouraged all who were enrolled in the correspondence courses, and answered their questions.

In those days, especially away from the major cities, slides were a crowd pleaser. To rest Art's voice during the evening presentations, Erma prepared a variety of slide sets with recorded narrative, showing aspects of the ministry of *Voce della Bibbia*, Trans World Radio in Monte Carlo, the activities of churches in the Modena province, and slides on other subjects such as prayer, Bible study, personal devotions, family devotions, and missions. Special events such as the Wiens trip to help after Sicily's earthquake, were also put on slides. Following the slides, Art would open the meeting to questions, sometimes only a few minutes, but more often longer, hard to turn off. After the service, book sales went on until everyone was satisfied, and one happy preacher was very, very tired.

Back at the host house, the discussions continued on into the night. 'And,' he recalls, 'the man of the house usually wanted me up for breakfast with him at 6:30 or 7:00, before he went to work!'

Twice in one trip, someone broke into Art's car and took everything of value. He lost the money from the book sales, his slide projector and irreplaceable slides, and other things the thief wanted. This type of vandalism was new to Italy, shocking to everyone. The second time there was not much left to take, except his suitcase of clothes. The police found it later. The thief had rifled through it and taken Art's razor, missed the first time!

Along with the ministry of encouragement visiting scattered churches, Art also introduced the Gideon program. His interest in doing this began in 1952, when the president of the California Gideons, Roy Parsons, came to Italy and spent a few days with Art and Erma. Art and Roy went to the director of the largest hotel in Florence to ask if they might place New Testaments in each room. He angrily told them that no Protestant scriptures could ever enter the hotels of Italy. Roy was challenged to ask Gideons in America to pray for a change in Italy.

The change started with the Ecumenical Council (1963-65). Pope John XXIII asked all Catholics to read the Bible fifteen minutes a day. As we noted earlier, a spirit of freedom of religious activity followed this council.

From 1973 to 1975 Lars Dagson, the European representative of the Gideons came three times to the Modena church to tell of their ministry. Gianni Iacobbe, a young financial consultant who had just been saved, was touched by the challenge and that evening plans were made to start the camp in Modena. Since they didn't have the minimum of six men in their church, they reached out to qualified Christian business men in Bologna, Reggio Emilia, and Mantova. Thus in 1977 one of the first Gideon camps in Italy was started in Modena. Today there are forty-six Gideon camps.

New Testaments are now placed in hotels and where possible in prisons and hospitals. Since they are not allowed to give them out in schools and universities in Italy, the Gideons notify the school director of their presence, but give out New Testaments on the sidewalks in front of the schools.

In Modena, they are also given out at the Military Academy. The Milan camp celebrated a huge victory in 1999. One of the men took a New Testament to a prisoner. When the secretary checked them in she asked who they were. When she heard they were Gideons, she asked them to bring 5,000 New Testaments to be placed in all four big prisons in Milan! It was a first for Italy!

As he traveled to churches, Art often mentioned the ministry of the Gideons, urging men of the church to take up this ministry. Christian workers are not allowed to be Gideons, but because of his tireless efforts in encouraging others, Art was named a consultant and travels with Italian Gideons to the Gideons International Conventions.

In addition to those mentioned, there were several outstanding conversions during the 1970s not related to radio outreach. Operation Mobilization had a tent set up in Reggio Emilia. One day when Renzo Creola and his wife were shopping there, he spotted it. Renzo challenged an OM missionary, 'You can't preach the gospel in a tent!'

'We do it all the time,' replied the young man. 'Come on in!' Creola said no, and remarked that he was from the town of Carpi. 'We're coming there next month,' said the missionary.

Carpi is in the region famous for sweater factories. Creola, who owned one, was very wealthy, and very Roman Catholic. He donated heavily to build Catholic hospitals and they kept several guest rooms so distinguished Catholic leaders could stay there en route north. During an illness in his youth, he had read 600 Catholic biographies hoping to become saintly. Once a month he had a Mass said in his factory and paid all his workers to attend, and he visited shrines regularly.

The Creolas attended the Carpi tent evangelistic meeting,

173

parking their big Mercedes next to the old OM truck. The speaker was Deliso Corradini, a friend of Remo's who was also a very strong speaker. He said he had planned to speak on parables, but the Holy Spirit had directed him to change his message, and instead, he spoke on six reasons why he had the assurance of salvation.

At the invitation, Creola started to get up. 'I'm going forward,' he whispered to his wife.

'If you do, I'll divorce you!' she snapped back. He sat down again.

That night Creola read the Bible all night long. He kept coming to tent meetings, and soon started attending a Bible study in a home in Carpi. The churches in Modena and Reggio Emilia took turns, one this week, the other the next. They said nothing about Sunday services. One night he asked what the believers did on Sunday. They told him, and he began attending. He spent several hours of a day in Bible reading and prayer, opening the mail at his office, and then settling down to his devotions. He also avidly read Christian books. Watchman Nee was his favorite author. He read 'The Normal Christian Life' many times!

Mrs. Creola did everything in her power to change his mind, bringing many influential leaders of the Catholic church to try to sway him. It was to no avail. After several months he was baptized, amid terrible family protests. For nine years he prayed fervently for his wife and children to be saved. At prayer meeting and at church on Sunday, he prayed publicly for them. Finally, she began to come with him, and at prayer meeting one night, she prayed publicly, asking God to forgive her and for her husband and the church to forgive her. She wanted to live for God as her husband did. There was hardly a dry eye when she finished praying.

Art and Erma believed that it was important for their

174

children to become American citizens. Since the U.S. required five years residence for this, in 1971, Shirley flew to New York to enter Columbia Bible College. The first year, she was so homesick that one day she looked up an Italian name in the phone book and spoke Italian to the man who answered! He happened to teach Italian and was happy to speak to her! After a break spending the summer in Italy, the second year she wrote back excitedly, 'My roommate is a girl from Italy! Yes, yes! Try to imagine who!' It was Debbie Martin, the daughter of missionaries in Naples, who was just as happy to find Shirley there. 'My joy is immense,' concluded Shirley.

Although she graduated with her Bachelor's degree 'Cum Laude', and returned for graduate work as a Resident Assistant, the remaining years were not exactly happy college days. She would have preferred to enter an Italian university with her school friends. Raised an Italian, and with limited exposure outside the missionary environment, she struggled with the American culture. Her heart was in Italy. She received her American citizenship, but at a great price. After a break with ill health, she went back to classes and completed her Master's thesis, returning home in November 1976.

While Shirley was away, a high school friend, Claudio Simonini had been studying for his degree in electronic engineering. They announced their engagement in the Spring of 1977, with plans for a June wedding. Gloria, leaving for CBC in the fall, was the excited bridesmaid. Daniel was six years old.

Chapter 11

Those Terrible 80s

The success of the Wiens' ministry was due in a large part to their 'saved to serve' philosophy. They understood that the best method for reaching the unreached was to train Italians to witness to their own people. To accomplish this, they drew people into their inner circle, even into their home and family life, where newcomers could learn by example, becoming an intregal part of the whole ministry. One didn't work for Art and Erma, one worked with them.

The people to whom they were called were educated and self-supporting. Missions had traditionally been among poor people in third world countries. Pioneers often learned the language by hiring unemployed, even illiterate persons to coach them. Missionaries had raised the living standards in many tribes through offering the only jobs available. With the help of their employees, they put unwritten languages into writing, and taught illiterate adults to read. Many missionaries went on from that point to hire assistants to translate the Bible and hymns into the local language. The result was a 'colonial father' image.

Missionary work in Italy began from an entirely different base. They were dealing with professional people, engineers, college students, business owners, and the children of people well-off enough to send their kids to camp. Everyone was literate, and reading material filled libraries, bookstores, and newsstands. In a nation of avid readers, even factory workers were self educated and diligent. And, contrary to third world nations, the missionaries were not rich (and therefore powerful), but average middle class folks.

In such a setting, gaining conversions was the hard part. Once a few people were saved and taught the basics of the Christian walk, the church planted could be indigenous, encouraged by more mature Christians of whatever nationality, but led and supported by Italians. This was the Wiens' goal, and the principle by which they lived.

God often uses a crunch of one kind or another to accomplish His purposes. In the case of church planting in Modena province, the housing shortage moved people around like checkers on a board, to places where God needed them. Dick and Beverly Mosher, veteran missionaries from Naples, came to help at *Voce della Bibbia* for a time. They commuted in from Carpi, where they found housing. After almost twenty years of living at Mrs. Marani's in a large house with a big yard (the third floor was theirs), the Wiens family had to move. Mrs. Marani had often hinted that she needed the apartment for her daughter's family, but the son-in-law assured them that he had no intention of moving there. When she got cancer, this changed. After much prayer and searching, Art and Erma found a seventh floor condominium in a large, modern building. It was on the outskirts of town, so the balcony overlooked a cornfield, destined to become a park. Daniel found friends his age there, and they soon adjusted to the new lifestyle.

Just the opposite, the Marinelli family moved from their apartment to a home they built in Formigine, seven miles from the office. They opened their new home to a Bible study for the many believers in that town. However, sadness clouded their lives when Rossana's third baby was found to have cystic fibrosis. Dr. Marinelli believed that the friendship and prayer support of the Modena church helped Rossana through this very difficult time. In nothing short of a miracle, Emanuele's health improved as medication allowed his body to absorb food, and the disease never invaded his pulmonary functions. Rossana's hours at the office were limited, but her special touch in the youth paper continued.

While the housing shortage gave the Bible studies at Carpi and Ostiglia a boost, Vignola, where the Casolari's lived when they were first married, received another couple willing to begin bi-weekly Bible studies in their home. Ellero, who lived at Formigine after his marriage, was a leader in the Modena church, but he helped a struggling little church at Maranello, as well as offering support to the Formigine group. Formigine was about to become a large, thriving church.

The steady growth of the radio ministry in nineteen years pushed out the walls of even the largest rented office space. Thirty people were involved in the work, twenty in the office and ten others collaborating in other ways. In 1980, *Voce della Bibbia* provided a daily 60-minute program called 'Living Water' to many Christian radio stations. A 15-minute program was released weekly on other stations. The correspondence, follow-up visitation, and literature ministry kept pace. But although there was much more that could be done, no more expansion was possible without new facilities. The first idea was to rent a warehouse and adapt it to suit their needs, but they abandoned the rental plan as a bad risk.

In a big step of faith, *Voce della Bibbia* announced a building project. The cost was expected to be $300,000, a phenomenal amount for those days. Back to the Bible trusted God for the funds needed for a 'revolving loan' to cover the largest portion of the project.

Land outside Modena city limits was about half the price, so they bought property at Formigine. They hoped to have the frame structure up by September 1980, at which time a 'Mission Tec Team' of volunteers from abroad would arrive to do the interior finish work and build the studios. This was a huge cost-cutter. Since Arthur planned to be in Kansas City for a Field Director's meeting at GMU, Back to the Bible asked him to extend his visit to contact friends and churches to personally present this important project. Funds for the 'Italy Building Project' began to come in both to GMU and to Back to the Bible.

The Wiens family (including Aunt Betty) took time off to celebrate the birth of Shirley's first baby, a little boy named Stefano. Several of the young couples were swelling the congregations at churches here and there about the same time, a very joyous event each time the news came in.

They broke ground for the new building on May 11, 1980. The ceremony was a praise service, spending time just thanking the Lord for the blessing *Voce della Bibbia* had been, and for His developing such an outreach all over Italy. The building permit was granted in record time and a Christian company from Asti was hired to erect the prefab shell. The company was owned by friends of *Voce della Bibbia.*

As the work began and the building started to take shape, the whole project seemed to be a formidable challenge. Timing was so important, since the 'Tec Team' was scheduled to arrive and it was important that building materials be on hand, the schedule be maintained, and the project continue to progress with harmony. The whole team, joined by interested folks around the world, bathed the project with prayer.

In November, 1980, Erma introduced the current *Voce della Bibbia* staff in the Wiens prayer letter:

'Robyn, from Australia, grew up in Taiwan as an MK. She does secretarial work and tape duplication. She is engaged to Gary, an MK from Ecuador who specializes in electronics and does program production. Sauro is a singer-composer and works in both music and program production. Anna is responsible for the work flow in mailing correspondence courses and other outgoing mail. Edda helps Anna with mailing and correspondence courses. (She had to put off her wedding due to the housing shortage!) Perside has been our accountant for six years. Daria does secretarial work and helps Erma with the youth magazine and calender. Ettore is office manager. Alberto works part time as artist and in graphics.

'Gianfranco and Marco are disc jockeys for one-hour daily programs. Each program involves the preparation of a four or five page script. Their continual deadlines create a lot of pressure. Frank King came to help us for three years with music production, but is currently very involved in the building project. His wife Kathy, mother of four children, is responsible for organizing meals for the builders and does a good share of the cooking. Remo, the counselor for seventeen years, prepares two preaching programs a week. Angela is Remo's wife and works in mailing. Betty works in mailing part time.

'Dave from Nebraska directs the radio work and the office. More than anyone else he needs to be upheld by prayer, as he is under a great deal of stress as he tries to keep things moving smoothly ahead in the office, at the studio, and on the building site. Dave and Judy Hansen have two boys, ages 5 and 2. Judy helps in the office one day a week. Rossana works part time on the youth paper.'

About seven of the volunteers with the Mission Tec Team were women. Some of them helped at the building site when they could. They all helped Kathy with feeding the crew at Formigine. Sunday dinners for the volunteers were at the Wiens' home.

All of this intense activity may have obscured a growing

problem in the Modena Church. In 1972, with a loan from Jim and Betty Hanna, the church purchased the two store fronts adjoining the original rented hall, and eventually also bought the rented portion. The expansion made room for eighty people. By 1981, this hall, too, was filled.

The Hanna's were Americans sent by the Campbell Soup Company to their Parma facility, where he was in charge of quality control. Although the drive from Parma was about 35 miles, the Hanna came to church at Modena every other Sunday. Jim Hanna was a Wheaton graduate who located Art Wiens in the Alumni Directory. He attended seminary and was a pastor before going to Campbell Soup Company. During the years he was at Parma, he often preached at Modena with Erma as interpreter, giving good, practical messages.

The believers repaid Mr. Hanna's loan, and his boost gave the church the motivation it needed to grow. But in 1980, just when things seemed to be going so well, an undercurrent of unhappiness developed.

King Solomon spoke in Ecclesiastes of 'the little foxes that spoil the vines'. Little issues so often lead to disagreement, and disagreement to argument, and argument to strife. It is no secret that the devil works overtime to weaken God's work where he sees success.

Several small irritations arose. Everyone should have rejoiced that the Lord had brought enthusiastic young men to the congregation. It seemed, however, that one elder had a problem with them preaching. His sour attitude caused some dissension. Arthur and Erma were on a summer furlough, but Erma returned first to get the children in school. Women did not attend business meetings, but the grapevine brought news. When Arthur arrived, she said, 'I think there are some difficulties.'

Even in America during the seventies and eighties, women who wore slacks or pant suits very cautiously began to test the waters at church. People stared, frowned, gossiped and wondered about women daring enough to break the dress code.

In Modena, an athletic young lady who accepted the Lord always wore slacks to church. She knew nothing about dress codes. She just discovered the truth, grew in understanding, and loved to meet with God's people. Her request for baptism ignited a spark that quickly grew into a smoldering inferno. Most of the elders felt that she should be baptized. One was against it. He brought out ample scripture to prove that women should not wear men's clothing, should dress modestly, and should learn from the older women how to dress. Instead of accepting her, it was the responsibility of the elders to confront her on this issue.

But he stood alone as the other side believed that in God's sight, it was the heart searching for Him that mattered, and that they should be praising the Lord that this young woman wanted to follow Him.

The majority ruled, but the dissenting elder didn't come to the baptism. For a year he sat in the back row at church, refusing to take part. Even when influential men begged him to preach, he refused. Art and Erma visited him, talked, pleaded, prayed, hoping for some change of heart. Other elders, too, tried to reason with him. People wrote him letters. His mind was set, and his insistence that his was the biblical view began to gather supporters. They agreed that he was right as to the letter of the law. He did know the scriptures. One Sunday in 1981, thirty people, including the unhappy elder, did not show up. They had started meetings of their own in a home elsewhere in the city.

The tension of the disagreement had been demoralizing to

the congregation. The unhappy mood grieved the Holy Spirit and saddened the group, putting a damper on their worship and prayer. When the remaining believers realized the implications of this final move, they were stunned. Relations remained strained as the two groups tried to sort out their own feelings and to find the mind of Christ. There was room for two churches in a city the size of Modena. Division of a large church was a good thing, and they could work things out. But the manner in which the division was made broke hearts and cast the remaining church leaders on the Lord for cleansing, renewal, and courage to go on.

During the summer of 1981, the staff of *Voce della Bibbia* moved into the completed new building 'by installment', finally getting everything from one location to the other. The time-consuming job was to get things in order once they were in, but eventually everything was set up and ready for action. Erma's mother and sister Ruth Plato came from Canada late in the summer, and Ruth put her decorating touches on the entrance and other hallways. They bought large wallpaper murals and divided them into three parts properly spaced on the long wall. These they framed with molding. Ruth left, but Erma and Gloria completed the job. In a brief vacation at the sea, Ruth and Erma made several macrame plant hangers to add an elegant touch of greenery.

That summer, Professor Artini, such a strong, godly leader in the Italian church, went home to be with his Lord.

Art and Erma Wiens made plans to take a furlough in the summer of 1982. In May, while they were wrapping things up in preparation for their trip, their whole world seemed to fall apart.

Such an immense organization as *Voce della Bibbia* had become needed to set parameters. Back to the Bible's ministry was radio, while Art and Erma's ministry was multifaceted – church planting, visitation, literature, camps, and radio all administered from the radio office. The dual ministry had become too broad, the activity under one roof too varied for efficient management. Both GMU and Back to the Bible, partners in this whole twenty-year venture, had the goal of indigenous work. Back to the Bible planned to turn all of their overseas offices over to national workers. In Italy, qualified people were available.

There was no easy way to tell Arthur and Erma Wiens that they were being terminated. Their ministry with *Voce della Bibbia* was over.

In retrospect, they could later explain to their families, donors, and friends that Back to the Bible Broadcast would be discontinuing the literature ministry except for radio supplements and counseling literature. GMU would be broadening its church planting ministry. There was still a dearth of evangelical literature in Italy, despite the huge amounts printed over the thirty years. Back to the Bible encouraged GMU to continue publishing efforts, including the youth magazine, Scripture Calendar, and study books. Back to the Bible also continued the monthly financial support for the Wiens that they had carried even before the Wiens entered radio.

June 5, Art and Erma flew to Los Angeles for a 'Narramore Professional Training Seminar for Counseling for Ministers and Missionaries'. Planned long before their paralyzing blow, the seminar messages helped to begin the healing process, and allowed them the necessary hours of introspection and grieving before tackling their furlough responsibilities. From there they went to Colorado for a Wiens Family reunion. As if to encourage His disheartened children, when they reached GMU the Lord had a new church-planting couple at the mission headquarters to meet

184

them. Phil and Sylvia Schroeder were on their way to Italy.

In Kansas City Art and Erma began the routine physicals, Art was hospitalized for more extensive tests. While there was some blockage in his arteries, it was not enough to cause pain. Then came another knock-out blow! On July 13th, as he was being given the 'Bernstein' test to examine the stomach, something went terribly wrong. Some of the liquid hydrochloric acid got into his lungs! They called a 'code blue' and began frantically working with him, and as his doctor said, 'It was touch and go for a few minutes!'

For two days Art was on a respirator in intensive care, and then on oxygen. The lungs did not recover as quickly as they hoped; some sections of the lungs were not functioning.

Erma, Gloria, and Daniel settled into a small apartment at the mission headquarters. Erma wrote, 'At times like these, when our plans are changed, we are inclined to listen carefully to all that God has to say. We recognize that there seems to be a pattern of trials and difficulties that has characterized our lives over the past months. What does it mean?'

Then she reflected back to twenty-five years before, when they were struggling to obtain visas to return to Italy. 'Immediately following each difficulty we were led into such exciting things for God!'

Arthur was released from the Kansas City hospital August 9th. When he was able to travel, Erma took him to California, where he became an outpatient at City of Hope. He was feeling good, but the incapacitated areas of the lungs made him cough, and he had difficulty speaking. A pulmonary specialist hoped to find a way to improve that area of his health.

At this point, Erma saw two options before them. Art was sixty and in ill health; she was six years younger, filled with boundless energy. They could retire, with minimal responsibility. Many folks do that. 'But,' she wrote, 'there are others who enter the most exciting and productive years of their lives at our age. If this is God's will for us, we'd rather be part of the latter category, making the most of our time.'

Erma and the children flew to Italy after Christmas, leaving Arthur in California. She rented the former *Voce della Bibbia* office space to open a bookstore and began making the necessary arrangements to do so, including writing for the necessary permission. Gloria's remaining classes at CBC were scheduled for the Spring quarter, so she could help her mother for a few weeks.

Instead of entering Italian high school, Daniel went to Black Forest Academy, a school in Germany for missionary children. His parents were concerned about the strong communistic influence in the Modena schools. 'During the cold war years Italy had the largest Communist party outside the Soviet Block countries,' explains Daniel. 'The Modena area was and still is the bedrock of Italian communism. My parents were afraid that I might be influenced by Communist ideology.'

Daniel was twelve years old, and after six years in the Italian school system, and spending the first half of his seventh grade in Pasadena, he went to BFA. He was about to have a rude awakening.

'After a few months living with a missionary family there, I went into the dorm. I was very spoiled at home. I had four moms: my real mom, Aunt Betty, Shirley, and Gloria. What I wanted, I got. It was tough adjusting to a dorm with forty other guys!'

Daniel feels that spending five and a half years in an international boarding school with Mks from all over Europe gave him a unique international perspective on life. 'My

186

sisters and I have settled in Italy because my folks met here, married here, and we were born here. Home always was Italy, not North America.'

The Hanna family, who spent a few years in Italy with the Campbell Soup Company, opened their home in Philadelphia to all the Wiens children for college years. Dan chose to attend Philadelphia Bible College, and upon graduation, returned 'home' to Italy.

Arthur was ready to meet Erma in Kansas City for deputation during the spring and summer of 1983. He left Pasadena on a summer-like day in February driving east, but he ran into stormy winter weather and icy roads in Kansas. He pushed on, hoping to reach Liberal, where his niece Marilyn lived. Driving was a struggle, and the weather won. Art tangled with a semi-trailer truck, demolished his car, and found himself back in the hospital.

Rather than meeting in Kansas City, Erma found Art at the Southwest Medical Center in Liberal, Kansas. They did finish the deputation planned for the previous year, before heading back to Italy. Because of his lung condition, it became necessary to leave Modena, so they rented a duplex at a mountain town 21 miles away. They chose Serramazzoni, altitude 2800 ft., above the fog of Modena. They could commute to the office, but on bad days, Arthur could work at home.

Serramazzoni was a resort town, with a small population of year-around residents. Winters were quite cold in this mountain town, and heavy snows fell. Heating was very expensive, so some merchants had no heat in their shops. They bundled up in sweaters and coats, and even wore gloves with a couple of fingers cut out so they could write. People in older homes heated only one room in the house, the big sitting room next to the kitchen, which generally had a huge fireplace. During the winter when tourists were few, to cut down on expenses the town used very few street lights.

In Italy, moving is a bigger adventure than it is in America. Along with everything else, they disconnect light fixtures and take them along, and built-in cupboards move from home to home, as well. Erma handled the electrical connections and got help with removing and reinstalling the cupboards her father had built years before.

The Wiens' duplex was a brand new home with no landscaping done. Even before the windows were in, Erma scouted for a good buy on wallpaper, and with the help of her sister Ruth and friend Betty Jabs who camped there with her for a few days, papered the entire three-bedroom house. Ruth helped the landlord plan the landscaping, and put in lovely professional flower gardens with roses and hanging baskets for Erma.

The kitchen and bath had beautiful Mediterranean ceramic tile on floors and walls. The floors in the rest of the house were also tiled, soft rose/ brown tones upstairs, and yellow tones in the large basement 'rumpus room'. At an auction in Canada, Ruth bought several large bolts of expensive upholstery material for forty dollars. Swatches of the material showed that it was a good match. With the help of some friends in Canada, she sewed quilted bedspreads and made drapes, and then came to Serramazzoni to complete the job, upholstering headboards and making cushions for benches at the end of each bed.

The following summer Ruth Plato, stressed out on her school-teaching job, requested a leave of absence. She returned to Italy, where she and Erma went to work stripping and refinishing their old furniture. The big project was coming along fine until one day Erma found a lump in her breast. It proved to be malignant. Art and Ruth went with her to the hospital, where in a small room just off the waiting area, a lumpectomy was unceremoniously performed. In about 20 minutes, Erma emerged with the doctor, her upper body covered with the hospital gown. She went home with no instructions, but the breast swelled terribly, so she returned to the doctor. When he removed the bandage, he found a very serious infection.

Leaving Ruth to work on alone at the house in Serramazzoni, Erma and Arthur flew to Kansas City, where she underwent a modified radical mastectomy. While she was still in the hospital, she also had carpel tunnel surgery in both wrists. Ruth recalls that after six weeks, Erma returned cheerful and ready to plunge back into her work.

A three-month old Gypsy girl was abandoned at the Sassuolo hospital, where she remained until she was nine months old, but no foster home was found. Since her husband was a doctor there, Rossana Maranelli asked Claudio and Shirley to take her in as a foster child. To Shirley's delight, her husband said yes. She was about a year and a half old when their daughter Cristina was born. In order to spare her the trauma of leaving the 'parents' she had grown to love, they asked to adopt her. After three years the court contacted them and granted the adoption, agreeing that little Simona should not be moved.

Gloria and some of her friends distributed leftover copies of *Il Tragaurdo* in front of various schools, and in the process, gave one to Mario Pieri's sister, Franca. The magazine carried an offer for a free year's subscription, so she sent for it. One day she told Mario that young evangelicals were coming to visit her. He came home just as they were finishing their visit, but he heard enough to make him under-stand that they had what he was searching for. As a result of that contact, both Mario and his sister accepted Christ.

Gloria and Mario met at church, while she was home from CBC one summer. They corresponded, and he visited her in America to meet her extended family the summer her father was hospitalized. In 1982 Mario, feeling called to serve the Lord, left a very good job to work as a technician at *Voce della Bibbia*. He and Gloria were married September 1984 and settled in Modena.

Serramazzoni was closer to the mountain town of Pavullo than it was to Modena, but Art and Erma decided to continue attending the Modena church, where they had been so long. The church was growing; the building had room for 80 chairs, but as many as 120 were attending. Erma got on the phone and called fifteen agencies, and finally located a building with about five times as much space as the current church. The new building was listed at $67,000, but they were offered only $17,000 for their hall. Although the elders and many of the church members saw it and liked it, they could not move ahead unless they got the money.

The church held fellowship dinners occasionally, which they called Agapes', or love feasts. One Sunday after the feast an elderly lady came in to ask Giorgio Ferrari (by that time one of the elders) if their hall was for sale. She took care of handicapped people and was looking for a place on the ground floor with double doors wide enough for a car to drive in. She was very anxious to get the hall owned by the evangelical church.

Giorgio called Art, who also talked to her. She offered to pay $50,000, plus closing costs of $5,600 if they would sell it. This was more than three times their best offer. It didn't take long for the elders to make their decision. They took a special offering, and came up with $23,000, $6,000 over the remaining amount to complete the purchase.

It was a win-win agreement. The disabled had a

wonderful new facility on Peretti Street, and the church moved to its new spacious location. Since the churches are identified by the street on which they are located, it became the Via Di Vittorio Church.

In 1989 Erma underwent another radical mastectomy. Thankfully, the decade of the 80s was over!

Chapter 12

CEM – The Modena Evangelical Center

Urgent personal matters seemed to consume Art and Erma Wiens for almost a decade, requiring several trips to the United States and including a major household move out of Modena after thirty years. The new building into which they moved took hours of time to get it ready, and their health problems would have stopped many people from even considering working outside the home. They were incredibly resilient and totally professional. The Lord's work remained foremost in their minds, and through it all, the show did go on.

While Arthur was still in rather frail health after his two accidents, Erma took the lead in setting up the new facility, which they named 'Centro Evangelico Modenese' (CEM), the Modena Evangelical Center. They were back in familiar quarters, the former *Voce della Bibbia* office, emptied of its furniture during the move to the new building. Erma began a search for office furniture, but as usual the Lord was one step ahead of her. A company that was replacing all their office furniture was disposing of the old. At a wonderful price they purchased five large desks, two small typing tables, several cabinets, seven office chairs, light fixtures (as mentioned earlier, the light fixtures are taken when one moves), and other useful items. Little by little the office took shape. As they reorganized, Arthur picked up responsibilities as director of CEM.

Planning their budget showed that they needed to raise $1,000 a month to pay the rent and running expenses of the office, as well as funds to subsidize the youth magazine. Personal support had gone up because of inflation, plus Daniel was in boarding school ($175 a month), and Gloria needed support for the year she planned to work at CEM. Erma wrote, 'Through these 33 years in Italy in His service, the Lord has always provided for every need.' She couldn't help but remember the first big challenge they faced in Florence.

They were two rather penniless young missionaries, living on Art's single status income, since Erma lost her support when she left her mission. Every month was an exercise in faith, but God took care of them The big test came when Shirley was born – they didn't have the money to pay the midwife – $8.00. On that same day, a check came in the mail from someone who just felt led to send a little gift. It was the exact amount needed!

Surely He 'who owns the cattle on a thousand hills' would see that CEM was properly funded. And, of course, He did.

The center was to be the hub of GMU's literature outreach, serving the immediate area with a bookstore and servicing more distant areas of northern Italy by mail order books and Bibles. CEM was also responsible for the publishing of children's books and other literature, and was the storehouse for remainder stock of books published prior to their opening. The youth magazine *Il Traguardo* remained their responsibility until Erma decided it was time for younger national workers to take it over. It was transferred to the Brethren Publishing House where it continues to be a testimony to youth throughout Italy. The Scripture Calendar was their major focus, a very exacting and time-consuming job, with tight schedules which had to be kept on track. The

193

Scripture Calendar also required a great deal of correspondence to and from potential users.

They were not alone. Betty Jabs (with her young charge Danny at the Black Forest Academy) was free to devote her time to the new venture. She was well experienced from working with Erma in the former office. Betty was versatile enough to fit in wherever she was needed. Her main responsibility became the mail room. In addition to mailing the youth magazine and the calendar, Betty prepared the packages of books and calendars that were ordered by mail.

While in college, Gloria felt called by the Lord to work with her parents at CEM. Like Shirley, Gloria had many of her mother's talents and was familiar with the procedures. Her bilingual skills as well as experience she had gained over the years made her a valuable employee. Even after her marriage to Mario Pieri, she was available to help with some of her specialties, preparing the youth magazine, graphics, proof reading, and the mailing list, which was now on computer.

Dick and Beverly Mosher, living in Carpi, supported the Wiens' new enterprise. They commuted to the Via Di Vittorio church in Modena, where Dick often preached. He and his son Paul took over one of the biggest jobs facing Art and Erma at CEM. They needed strong metal storage shelves in their warehouse. To keep them steady with the weight of heavy books stacked on them, the shelves needed to be anchored to the wall. Dick and Paul worked steadily on this project until the warehouse was ready to receive literature.

Abe and Mary Unrau returned to Italy and as it worked out, after they brushed up on their Italian in Florence, they were able to rent the condominium the Wiens vacated when they moved to the mountains. With the housing shortage, this was an answer to prayer, especially as they considered the

194

central location. It was ideal for reaching the whole area. Because of their maturity and past experience in Italy, and Abe's experience as a pastor in Canada, they were a wonderful addition to the team and a big encouragement to the Wiens. The little church at Maranello was struggling, but Abe was able to help there. Phil and Sylvia Schroeder were at Vignola.

In time, the rift between members of the two churches healed and they agreed to disagree agreeably. The roots of friendship between people in both congregations held firm even though their differences in interpreting some scripture passages kept the smaller church from meeting with Via Di Vittorio.

The staff at *Voce della Bibbia* were either former colleagues of Art and Erma, or folks who had grown up attending their youth group, Intervarsity, Evening Bible School, or camp activities. Friendships there remained firm.

The tie between the Via Di Vittorio Church and CEM was strong. At the time the church was divided, Giorgio Ferrari, Fabio Arini, and Arthur Wiens assumed the responsibility for carrying the heavy burden of regrouping and repairing the damage done. Along with their wives, the three couples met often for prayer during those difficult days.

Giorgio – just a teenager when Art met him in Sassuolo – and his wife Franca (whose radiant face brought Rossana Marinelli to Christ) were faithful helpers. Giorgio never preached, but his stability and quiet testimony spoke volumes. For many years he was the Treasurer of the church, and Franca the organist. The church began a prayer meeting before Sunday morning service, which the Ferrari's often attended, and they were always at the regular Thursday night prayer meeting. Franca frequently said to Arthur after a prayer meeting, 'Isn't the Lord good?'

From the time Fabio Arini (the professor of gymnastics) first heard the gospel he had a hunger to know the Word of God. His wife Perside (a blonde Italian) came to *Voce della Bibbia* from southern Italy to work as accountant, where she met Fabio. Fabio became director of the church radio work. An avid Bible student, once he began preaching, he gave excellent messages. Arthur says of Fabio, 'He prays more like Jim Elliot than anyone I have ever known!'

Fabio was a soul winner. He was burdened for his mother, who had a hunger for spiritual matters. His father, an atheist, was a Sicilian police officer. Whenever he was away, Fabio arranged for Erma to go have a Bible study with his mother. After she was saved and baptized, her husband didn't hinder her from joining in worship. His sister Daria was also a Christian.

Gildo Bernardi, another elder, was a mountain boy who fell in love with a visitor from Florence. Derna's father was a leader in their church in Pesaro. Derna, a Christian, got a job in Florence and was in the mountains for a wedding the weekend she met Gildo. She married this unsaved mountain boy, but was encouraged in her faith by *Zia Erma's* youth broadcasts, and attended Erma's Old Testament Bible studies. For about eight years the church joined Derna in prayer for her husband. Giorgio and Gianni did a Bible study in the Bernardi home, and finally, he accepted Christ as his Savior. Godfrey Miller carefully discipled Gildo, who loved getting up early in the morning to study the Bible and good Bible study books.

The testimony of Carlo Neri, another elder, is interesting. Brought up Roman Catholic, he and his wife were searching for the truth. The Jehovah's Witnesses were very strong in Modena, regularly going two by two to homes until they found one where they could hold a Bible study. Carlo and

Loretta followed them for a while, but became disillusioned. Next they tried the Mormons. They became disgusted with religion, and decided to have no more contact with any of the churches.

Carlo worked at a fresh fruit and vegetable warehouse. Loretta worked at home, sewing fur coats, so she could listen to the radio. One evening she said to Carlo, 'I've found religious programs I really like.'

'We decided not to follow any other religions,' he reminded her.

'I know,' she said, 'but these are really different.'

Carlo listened to the *Voce della Bibbia* programs and decided to go to Formigine to find out who these people were. He talked to a counselor for a while, and then asked, 'What if a couple fights?'

'My wife and I have difficulties now and then,' admitted the counselor, 'but before going to sleep we make it right and ask God's help.'

The Neris began attending church and Carlo was soon converted. He wanted to be baptized. 'Wait,' they told him, 'so you and Loretta can be baptized together after she is saved.'

He waited, and they were baptized together, along with Daniel Wiens.

Carlo became a well loved elder with a very caring spirit. Loretta was a special help to Daniel, who sometimes went to her with his problems.

Getting the license to open a bookstore took over a year. Although there was no evangelical bookstore between Florence and Milan, the authorities denied their request, saying there were enough bookstores in Modena. This required documentation to prove that a need for such a store existed.

Matters of this nature were usually turned over to another

faithful church elder, Gianni Iacobbe (Art calls him Johnny). Like his father before him, Gianni became a police officer. While in Milan he met a Modena girl and married her. They moved back to Modena.

Someone put a tract from Every Home Crusade in Gianni's mailbox. He did a correspondence course with them, and his name was sent to Arthur for follow up. Gianni was very busy, but for a year Arthur would drop into his office periodically for a brief visit. One day Gianni said to Arthur, 'I went to my priest to talk to him about birth control, and I wasn't happy with his answer. Could you help me?'

'Yes,' replied Arthur, 'But not here in your office. Your home, or mine.'

Arthur went to Gianni's home with a small booklet on birth control in his pocket. He handed it to Gianni, but the subject never was discussed. Instead Gianni told Arthur he was reading his Bible. They talked until midnight, and he invited Arthur back. Depending on their schedules, sometimes Art took Remo Dosi along for what turned out to be three years of bi-weekly in-depth Bible studies, and sometimes Remo went alone. Gianni took every Bible study to his priest. Art knew the priest well, and sometimes went with Gianni.

'The priest was a New Testament professor in a Roman Catholic seminary,' explains Art. 'He probably knew most of the New Testament by heart in Greek.'

After three years of this routine, Gianni stumped the priest. He couldn't explain how the bread and wine actually became the body and blood of Christ. This raised serious doubts in Gianni's mind, so he asked about evangelical services. He started coming and soon was baptized. He was especially fascinated by prophecy, which he studied rigorously, and when he started to preach, this was often his subject. His wife divorced him because he was too religious, and she soon had a new, very worldly boyfriend.

Gianni remarried, and Miria Iacobbe was a Christian. She went to London for a study vacation, and while she was there, she met a Christian professor who explained the gospel to her. He also told her that in Modena there was a good evangelical church. She attended one Sunday, and was immediately impressed with Erma, who showed such kindness and such personal interest in her. Miria accepted Erma's warm invitation to her Old Testament Bible study on Saturday evenings. After the studies, Daniel would come in his pajamas just as Erma was giving out sweets, delicious sweets that Miria knew must take a great deal of time to make. These contacts won her heart.

Gianni's job was with a financial consulting company. His work took him to Rome to update his information, and he knew all the right people in the right places. With Gianni's assistance, the license for the CEM bookstore was finally granted.

The location of the CEM office was not good for a bookstore, but shops on the best streets were too expensive to consider. In 1988 they located a store on a side street that, although not in the direct line of pedestrian traffic, was suitable. It took a special effort with a variety of publicity techniques to make the new location known.

As to publishing projects carried on by CEM, Erma's project in her last five years was to translate a series of thirteen children's books into Italian. These were done by co-edition, printed with the help of a British publisher in London, Angus Hudson.

In the fall of 1973, a representative of the Bible House of Geneva, Switzerland met Arthur for tea during an international book fair in Frankfurt, Germany. 'We have the

Scofield Bible in German,' he explained, 'and it is just being completed in French. What do you think about publishing it in Italian?'

The proposal sounded good to Art, so he replied, 'I'll take the idea to the *Voce della Bibbia* committee.'

If you want something done, they say, ask a busy man to do it. Of those who heard the proposal of the Bible House, Samuele Negri was the most vitally interested. Some of the Scofield notes had been printed in Italian, but were no longer in print. The following year a group was called together at the Wiens home to discuss the idea. Their conclusion was that before translating the Scofield notes, the Italian Bible needed to be revised.

The common Bible in Italy for many years was the 1607 edition of Giovanni Diodati. This was revised by Giovanni Luzzi and a committee in 1924. There had been many language changes in fifty years, and the 1924 edition had some doctrinal weaknesses. Samuele Negri along with a group of capable Italians and with the help of the British and Foreign Bible Society representative in Rome tackled the monumental task of a major revision. The revised Italian Bible was printed in 1994, with some helps. The Scofield Study Bible in Italian was scheduled to be printed by the Bible House of Turin, Italy, in the year 2000.

A two-volume Bible Knowledge Commentary is in progress, 2580 pages in English. It will be even larger in Italian. This translation, also supervised by Samuele Negri, is being done by various Italians skilled in the written language. CEM is the official publisher of the Bible Knowledge Commentary, but the printing will be done elsewhere.

The Scripture Calendar – almost the crown jewel of the Modena team – has had such a far reaching testimony. In about 1964, Erma arranged for a simple little calendar to be

200

sent for Christmas to the children listening to her program. It was very well received. From 1965 to 1971, they sent a calendar giveaway to the adult list each December. They were not happy with it, but couldn't think what to do to make a more useful and attractive product. One day they phoned the Negris. 'We have something special we'd like to talk over with you.' They arranged to get together.

In the meeting about the calendar, all agreed that something else should be done. But what? There was a French calendar translated into Italian with a scripture verse in fine print and, also in fine print, a meditation. When translated into Italian from French it was not entirely suitable. But it sparked an idea. Erma cried, 'A tear-off page, with a verse for each day in large letters on the front, and nothing on the back! People getting the calendar will see the new scripture verse – in plain bold letters – every time they tear off a day!"

It was decided to go ahead. Through Erma's skill in preparing the copy for printing, 2,000 copies were sent out in 1972. The comments were favorable, but most people wondered why the back side was left blank. Since the letters came to Remo Dosi in the counseling department, he wrote about 100 meditations for the following year.

Preparing the Scripture Calendar is now a year around job. Currently twenty-four writers are contacted each spring, given an assignment of certain verses for which they are to write a meditation. The writers are volunteers, their only reward the satisfaction of reaching out into the homes of unbelievers with a daily testimony from the Word of God. They range from professional writers to housewives, from professors to policemen. They are given out well in advance, usually with vacation time in mind, so the writers will not feel pressured.

Over the years, Erma prepared the calendar for the printer with the help of various graphic artists and other talented staff, including her two daughters. In 1992 she was diagnosed with bone cancer. She worked on until 1996. Young missionaries from Germany, Michael and Rosa Stoehr were coming to work in the literature ministry, and it was Erma's hope that her health would hold out so she would have plenty of time to lead Michael through the process. She wanted him to thoroughly learn the complicated process before he took over.

Things don't always go as planned. With great effort, she taught him what she could before her illness dictated that she stop. She was bedridden at her beautiful new home in Serramazzoni, her two best companions, Betty Jabs and Ruth Plato, at her side to care for her. Daniel was out of school and living at home. One of her last duties by phone from her sickbed was to approve a third edition printing of the Bible story book she had prayed for so long, and had seen become a reality.

The last Sunday, she slept all day. It was Daniel who came to his father's room the next morning to say, 'Mom is in heaven, Dad.'

Her send-off was superb, as fifty years' worth of friends came to say farewell, and to extend their love and sympathy to her family. Godfrey Miller, who took the funeral, felt compelled to open the meeting for spontaneous testimony. Many gave glory to God for the way Erma had touched their lives. He said of Erma, 'In her last months she was a revelation, teaching us all how a Christian prepares for death, as she had taught so many of us how a Christian ought to live.' She was laid to rest in the Protestant cemetery in Modena.

During the time Erma was facing her final illness, Silvano

and Liliana Casolari, missionaries in Pavullo, met her at the hospital one day. Silvano also had cancer. He passed away a few months after Erma.

Michael took over the responsibility of the calendar. He works two years in advance. The letter to potential buyers goes out in January asking how many calendar they want to order. They must respond by the middle of March. To take advantage of the early order discount the minimum order is 200. Small churches are advised to get together on their orders, if necessary. The printer in Germany is then notified of the total number of calendars they will need. All orders must be paid for by May 1 and will not be sent if not paid for in advance. To get the best price, the whole order, now nearly 140,000, must be sent to the printer in Germany during down time. Deadlines are firm.

Assignments to the writers must go out on time, and once the meditations come in, they must be carefully checked for doctrinal error, or other flaws.

Photocomposition is now done by computer. From beginning to end, it is exacting work. Proofreading and checking for accuracy is done time and again. The project must march along on schedule in order for the whole process to work.

Right at the start, the Lord gave Erma special wisdom to work out the shipping arrangements, which constitute a monumental task. Large orders come in from churches and bookstores all over Italy. The delivery from the printer arrives at the Modena railroad station in large trucks about the middle of May. Most are shipped directly to the customers from the railroad station the next day, after CEM places labels on the boxes and prepares the necessary shipping papers. To save shipping expenses (which the customer pays) some are picked up at the station. Small numbers (at higher cost) are shipped by the mailing department at CEM to those who requested them. About 10,000 are kept at the CEM bookstore for sale.

While he was visiting churches during the 1970s, Arthur would carry a supply of calendars to distribute to eighty or ninety Brethren Assemblies. He would encourage them to use the calendars for witnessing, and many people did take a supply. Later those copies were mailed or picked up by the churches, while he personally distributed in his own territory.

The Scripture Calendar is non-sectarian, just scripture verses, with meditations that challenge one to know God, His Word, and themselves. One tear-off page offers a Bible for sale. On November first there is a reorder coupon and a list of Christian bookstores is included. A few Catholic bookstores sell the Scripture Calendar. Perhaps in the daring of old age, Art began to send one to the Pope, who each time wrote an official thank you letter in return.

At age seventy-five, Arthur retired as director of *Centro Evangelico Modenese* (CEM). In the reorganization, the direction came under a committee of seven. Vince Chiaravallotti was chosen as the GMU representative on the committee. Vince and Roberta are church-planting missionaries under GMU living at Treviso, near Venice. Michael and Rosa Stoehr of the German Missionary Fellowship are both on the committee. He is the administrator of CEM. Gianni Iacobbe is valued in part for his adept handling of legal matters. Robert Malcolm, grandson of Abele Biginelli (who pioneered Christian literature production in Italy) is manager of the bookstore. Gloria Pieri (sensitive to the mind of her mother in decision-making), and Arthur Wiens make up the remainder of the committee.

As part of his job at *Voce della Bibbia*, Arthur's son-in-law Mario Pieri is manager of the local Christian radio station, *Radio Risposta*. Its main goal has always been to proclaim the gospel and since it is a non-commercial station it accepts no advertising, but looks to the Lord for finances. Funds come through Back to the Bible Broadcast in Lincoln, as well as from Italian donors. All of *Voce della Bibbia's* radio production (about four hours a day in radio programs) is distributed to about 20 Christian stations throughout Italy associated with FARE (Federation of the Evangelical Radio Association) including *Radio Risposta*. The added hours are filled with a combination of gospel music, Christian biographies and missionary stories read in installments, news, and Bible studies.

Shortly after Erma died, Arthur moved to an apartment that Mario and Gloria had prepared for her parents on the ground floor of their home. Art is still very active in his church and his witnessing ministry. Shirley and Daniel also live in Modena, so he enjoys family gatherings and his grandchildren: the Pieri boys who live upstairs, John and Matteo, and the Simonini children, Stefano, Simona, Cristina, and Laura. He still sets aside October through January to distribute Scripture Calendars personally. When he could no longer drive, he carried them everywhere he was able to go using Italy's excellent public transportation. Friends take him to special areas such as Serramazzoni, where he and Erma made so many friends. Everyone receives not only the calendar, but another personal witness from the missionary they have grown to love.

Despite the amazing growth of evangelical witness throughout all Italy, it is still a very needy mission field. Statistics show an increase in fifty years from ¼ of one percent of the population Protestant, to ½ of one percent!

Communism, cults, and the Catholic church contend for souls, but seem not to satisfy the hearts truly searching to know God. To those who pray for Italy, your brothers and sisters in the land send their heartfelt thanks. Prayer is their lifeline. They need the companionship of your daily, fervent prayer. To those who are called to sponsor missionaries, radio work, literature projects, and special efforts, as Erma Wiens would say, 'Thank you for being such a vital part of the team!' To those called of God to serve Him abroad, the people of this land so near Macedonia send a warm and sincere invitation, 'Come over and help us!'

And to tourists who come to see the sites of Rome, as you gaze in awe at the magnificent cathedrals, splendor of art collections, and wonderful ancient gardens remember that the greatest work of God in Italy was not done among the rich and mighty, but one on one, by a man under house arrest chained to a Roman guard.

That's the way God works! In surprising, exciting, and marvelous ways, He is still drawing people to himself in this land of searching hearts.

Christian Focus Publications publishes biblically-accurate books for adults and children. The books in the adult range are published in three imprints.

Christian Heritage contains classic writings from the past.

Christian Focus contains popular works including biographies, commentaries, doctrine, and Christian living.

Mentor focuses on books written at a level suitable for Bible College and seminary students, pastors, and others; the imprint includes commentaries, doctrinal studies, examination of current issues, and church history.

For a free catalogue of all our titles, please write to
Christian Focus Publications,
Geanies House, Fearn,
Ross-shire, IV20 1TW, Great Britain

For details of our titles visit us on our web site
http://www.christianfocus.com

About the Author

Evelyn Stenbock-Ditty spent twelve years as a missionary to Morocco with Gospel Missionary Union. Her career as an editor and staff writer at Nazarene Publishing House included serving as Associate Editor of *Come Ye Apart* and Program Materials editor for Lillenas Publishing Company. She has published several books, including *Teach Yourself to Write*, *"Miss Terri!"*, *A Gleam of Light*, and the Beacon Small-Group Bible Study on Ecclesiastes. She makes her home in Kansas City, KS.